A Social History of American Family Sociology, 1865-1940

Recent Titles in
Contributions in Family Studies

A Coat of Many Colors: Jewish Subcommunities in the United States
ABRAHAM D. LAVENDER, EDITOR

Passing: The Vision of Death in America
CHARLES O. JACKSON, EDITOR

Cross-Cultural Perspectives of Mate-Selection and Marriage
GEORGE KURIAN, EDITOR

A Social History of American Family Sociology, 1865-1940

RONALD L. HOWARD

With an additional chapter on Early Family Sociology in Europe by LOUIS TH. VAN LEEUWEN

Edited by John Mogey

CONTRIBUTIONS IN FAMILY STUDIES, NUMBER 4

GREENWOOD PRESS
WESTPORT, CONNECTICUT • LONDON, ENGLAND

306.8
H851s

Library of Congress Cataloging in Publication Data

Howard, Ronald L
  A social history of American family sociology,
1865-1940.

  (Contributions in family studies ; no. 4 ISSN
0147-1023)
  Includes bibliographical references and index.
  1. Family--Research--United States--History.
2. Family--Research--Europe--History. 3. United
States--Social conditions--1865-1918. 4. United
States--Social conditions--1918-1932. I. Leeuwen,
Louis Th. van, joint author. II. Mogey, John M.
III. Title. IV. Series.
HQ535.H63   306.8'0973   80-1790
ISBN 0-313-22767-5 (lib. bdg.)

Library of Congress Catalog Card Number: 80-1790
ISBN: 0-313-22767-5
ISSN: 0147-1023

First published in 1981

Greenwood Press
A division of Congressional Information Service, Inc.
88 Post Road West, Westport, Connecticut 06881

Printed in the United States of America   82-6771

10 9 8 7 6 5 4 3 2 1

CONTENTS

PREFACE

John Mogey

This book tells the story of how a group of scholars began to identify a common set of interests, then worked out an acceptance of common concepts. Certain methods of research developed using these concepts, leading these scholars to recognize themselves in a new identity. This, in turn, encouraged the search for scholarly and professional independence. In the course of this century, many new professional groups have emerged with increasing frequency, particularly in the borderlands between established sciences. Sociologists separated themselves from philosophers, historians and economists late in the nineteenth century. The borderland between practicing social reformers—concerned about deviant behavior such as crime, drunkenness, divorce, or desertion—social historians, and social statisticians came to be more and more the area where sociologists focused their writing. Among these sociologists those who took as their unit of social analysis the household or the family soon found that their problem area called for special concepts and methods. Sociologists writing about collective actions by governments or by religions, or writing about stratification or about broad historical changes in societies treated the family unit as something that responded to social change rather than as an important initiator of broad changes in Western societies. Family sociology separated very early in the emergence of sociologists as a scholarly profession. This book is about the way in which family sociology was begun.

To cover the creation of the new academic discipline of family sociology, both in the United States and in Europe, we have combined the major part of the dissertation of Ronald L. Howard, presented at the University of Missouri in 1975, with an essay specially written for this work. The accidental death of Ronald Howard, while he was revising his history for publication, means that this volume becomes his memorial, rather than marking the start of his career.

The American Sociological Association, Family Section, found the dissertation interesting and set up a subcommittee to make recommendations about publication. I write from the chair of this subcommittee. We invited Louis Th. van Leeuwen, Agricultural University, Wageningen, The Netherlands, to read the manuscript and advise us. He had in 1976 published a study of the history of family sociology in Europe.[1] Thanks to a fellowship from the American Council of Learned Societies, he was able to spend most of the academic year 1978-79 with me at Boston University. Other members of the subcommittee, Glen H. Elder, Jr., Cornell University; Reuben Hill, University of Minnesota; and Jetse Sprey, Case-Western University, assisted actively in decision making.

DECISIONS LEADING TO THIS PUBLICATION

The first decision was easy: the Howard manuscript was exceptionally well written and accurate in its major dimensions. The dissertation should be published as much as possible as the author intended, and in this way it would be a fitting memorial. Consequently, what we have done is to publish the Howard text covering the period up to 1940.

The period between 1940 and 1980 saw an outpouring of works in family sociology unlike anything that had gone before. The Inventory of Marriage and Family Literature shows that about 2 percent of the items in the English language appeared between 1900 and 1928; from 1929 to 1940, about 6 percent appeared; between 1941 and 1971, 67 percent appeared. In the years between 1972 and 1976, there appeared 25 percent of all articles and books. In other words, up to 1940, the historian had to deal with 10 percent of the publications: 90 percent of all existing family sociology has been written and published since 1940. The grand total for 1900 to 1976 is 25,557 items.[2]

One satisfactory way to deal with this flood of material is to use some form of citation analysis, a quantitative approach to data that was not available to a historian such as Howard. His techniques make excellent sense of developments between 1865 and 1940. These seventy-five years saw the emergence of a succession of creative individual scholars who stated the basic ideas needed to create the discipline of sociology. The present text elegantly shows how these ideas first appeared and the way they interacted with other ideas in several networks that made up the intellectual environment of that period. Sociologists were asked to apply these ideas to social problems in the first years of the existence of the discipline, and so family sociology began.

Although basic sociological concepts, such as structural supports for marriage and the family and interaction between individuals in their family roles, continued to be examined in numerous publications, after 1945 a multitude of new ideas were tried out by family sociologists. The topic Marriage and Divorce continues to be important, but its dominance as a topic for serious research has lessened progressively since 1900. Alongside it have risen studies of interaction within the family, whose beginnings with the work of G. E. Howard and Ernest Burgess are given in this text. Some indication of the rapid rate of change in topics is that, by 1975, counseling or therapy was the orientation of a majority of articles, closely followed by education.[3] Interest in individual outcomes rather than group effects clearly distinguishes family sociologists from others in the discipline of sociology, a difference that becomes visible in the period covered by this history.

The second decision was much more troublesome: the committee decided to omit rather than publish Howard's chapters on the period 1940-1969. Any editor would have wanted to add new interpretations, which would no longer have been the original text. Besides, the elegance of the Howard paragraphs, the way that

evidence is marshalled and used to present a compelling interpretation of the creative years of this new profession deserved to be
presented as the author had intended. The subsequent period
requires a separate volume to do it justice.

The third decision was to add to the developments in the United
States an additional chapter about European parallels. Howard
makes clear how selected European ideas penetrated into the formative years of American sociology. He refers at length to the influence of Herbert Spencer, to Florian Znaniecki and to the use of
Frédéric Le Play. Consequently, an account of the European work
in family studies, as a precursor to family sociology, not only adds
an international scope to this volume but also helps in the interpretation of trends in the United States.

The sociologist reader should be alerted at this point to expect that
footnotes in this book follow the style of the historians, rather
than that used in the social sciences. In effect, there are two books;
(1) the text as an organized series of arguments and (2) the footnotes
as a commentary on the sources used to construct the statements
in the text.

HISTORY, SOCIOLOGY, THEORY, AND THE FAMILY SOCIOLOGIST

The central idea Howard used to organize the analysis is that
family sociology is "an intellectual enterprise which interacts with
the society which contains it." This starts from a notion of Toulmin's that "ideas . . . exist within intellectual niches," but goes
beyond to specify, as the history unfolds, the interactions between
the members of the niches known as social reformers and those
known as sociologists as they compete for attention and support.[4]
The first great American work in family sociology began as a
contribution to social reform: this was "The Divorce Problem: A
Study in Statistics."[5] After 1900, social work and sociology diverged
quickly, although they both began in the same ferment of ideas at
the close of the nineteenth century.

Moral reformers were alarmists about trends and tended to propose
actions based on statements such as "to save the family is to save

society itself.'' The profession of social work took over part of this ideology, seeing the family as a fragile unit, needing protection and social support to prevent its disappearance in an urban world, where delinquency, desertion, divorce, and drunkenness were becoming increasingly noticed.

Sociologists, on the other hand, asked often by reformers and by governmental organizations to look for statistics that showed the decline of the family through divorce, found to the contrary that the family was adaptable, resilient, and very capable of adjusting to changes in its economic, moral, and social environment. The second great publication of the precursors, G. E. Howard's *A History of Matrimonial Institutions*, marked the beginning of a new theoretical paradigm, the use of social psychology as the theoretical perspective that enabled sociology to claim professional status and a new autonomy among the social sciences.[6]

The birth year for family sociology, as a separate branch of sociology, seems to have been 1924. Two events marked its birth. First, at Boston University, Ernest Groves began family life education, a movement that aimed at the preparation of college students for the responsibilities of marriage. He saw family education as the art of creating affection, the central value needed for continuity of any family as a social group. Second, at the American Sociological Society, the section on Family was begun. From this time forward, contributions on the family become more and more common in sociological journals. By 1935, Howard notes the journal article, rather than the book, as the sign that this specialized group of sociologists had an identity of their own. By 1937, they had their own professional journal, *Marriage and Family Living*, a publication of the National Council on Family Relations.

However, between 1920 and 1940, the most influential figure in family sociology was Ernest W. Burgess of the University of Chicago. He combined ideas from interaction and social psychology in such a way that he rescued the family from being considered simply one form of primary group. His concept of the family as a unity of interacting personalities and his emphasis on predictive research came to dominate the output of family sociology in the United States until at least 1955.

In the United States, a new scholarly profession, the family sociologist, had by 1940 its own field of study, its own theories and
methods of research, its interests in social policy, and its own
identity. This new niche was by then complete with meeting places
at special conferences and journals in which to publish research
findings. The members of this new profession were poised for the
great expansion of work on the family that followed the White
House Conference of 1948. This expansion, however, will require
a separate book, which is now being researched.

ACKNOWLEDGEMENTS

My debts to the members of the ASA Family Section subcommittee
are evident: they actively co-operated in all stages of the preparation.
The ACLS fellowship that made the visit of Dr. Louis van Leeuwen
possible was crucial to the enterprise. Extra photocopies of the
original were made by Felix Berardo, University of Florida, who
was secretary of the ASA Family Section in 1978. Boston University
Graduate School added a grant for typing. My wife, Doreen, typed
and improved a series of drafts and kept correspondence flowing.
The widow of the late Dr. Ronald Howard added her enthusiastic
support to this endeavor.
As editor, I acknowledge with gratitude the assistance of all who
made it possible to prepare this material for publication. Defects
and errors of judgment remain and are mine alone.

September 1980
Tempe   85281

NOTES

1. Louis Th. van Leeuwen, "Het gezin als sociologisch studie-object"
(Wageningen: Agricultural University, doctoral thesis: September 29, 1976).
2. David H. Olsen and Nancy S. Dahl, *Inventory of Marriage and
Family Literature, 1975 and 1976*, vol. 4 (Minneapolis: Family Social
Science, University of Minnesota, 1977); *Inventory of Marriage and Family
Literature, 1973 and 1974*, vol. 3. Joan Aldous and Nancy S. Dahl, *In-
ventory of Marriage and Family Literature, 1965-1972*, vol. 2 (Minneapolis:
Family Social Science, University of Minnesota, 1974). Joan Aldous and
Reuben L. Hill, *International Bibliography of Research in Marriage and*

the Family, 1900-1964 (Minneapolis: University of Minnesota Press, 1967).

3. Reuben Hill, "Sociology of Marriage and Family Behavior 1945-56: A Trend Report and Bibliography," *Current Sociology* 7, no. 1 (1958); John Mogey, "Sociology of Marriage and Family Behavior: A Trent Report and Bibliography," *Current Sociology* 17, nos. 1-3 (1969).

4. Stephen Toulmin, *Human Understanding* (Oxford: Oxford University Press, 1972), vol. 1: General Instruction and part 1.

5. Walter F. Willcox, *The Divorce Problem: A Study in Statistics*, Columbia University Studies in History, Economics, and Public Law, vol. 1 (New York: Columbia University Press, 1891).

6. George E. Howard, *A History of Matrimonial Institutions Chiefly in England and the United States with an Introductory Analysis of the Literature and the Theories of Primitive Marriage and the Family*, 3 vols. (Chicago: University of Chicago Press, 1904).

ABBREVIATIONS OF REFERENCES

AJS	*American Journal of Sociology*
Annals	*Annals of the American Academy of Political and Social Science*
ASR	*American Sociological Review*
JHBS	*Journal of the History of the Behavioral Sciences*
JMF	*Journal of Marriage and the Family*
MFL	*Marriage and Family Living*
NCCC	*National Conference of Charities and Correction*
NDRL Report	*Report of the National Divorce Reform League*
NLPF Report	*Report of the National League for the Protection of the Family*
S & S R	*Sociology & Social Research*
SF	*Social Forces*

A Social History
of American
Family Sociology,
1865-1940

INTRODUCTION

Ronald L. Howard_____

Few historical specialities have grown as rapidly as family history. From scattered works in the sociological literature through the first half of this century, the field burgeoned in the late 1960s and became a viable specialty in the 1970s. As an academic specialty, family history is notable for two striking characteristics: its international dimensions and its interdisciplinary approach and composition. Family history has not been confined within national boundaries, and American family historians interact with their foreign colleagues to a far higher degree than is true of other historical specialties. American family historians have used methodologies pioneered by French and English demographic historians and have collaborated with them in collective studies, the most notable being the Cambridge Group for the History of Population and Social Structure. Family history is also an interdisciplinary specialty. The field is not exclusively populated by historians, but includes as well sociologists, economists, anthropologists, and psychologists who have produced family history research. It is not a field where historians engage in research while other social scientists offer theoretical support. It is a genuinely collaborative specialty in which scholars from several social sciences contribute to a common body of theory and research.

Although the rapid growth of family history has led to the production of an impressive body of research about the family in

past time, scant attention has been paid by family historians to the
specialty of family sociology, the major forum of family theory and
research during the twentieth century. The study of this academic
speciality is important, for it can provide scholars of the family
with an understanding of the growth and diversity of research on
the family that has already been done. Family sociologists have
been accused, with some justice, of neglecting the historical dimensions of their research object. Family historians, however, can
equally be faulted for failing to devote the same attention to the
development of family theory and research that they have given to
census data, town records, diaries, and tombstones. Family sociology, as a discipline, has generated an enormous amount of research
that, with the passage of time, has become historical data. As such,
it too is grist for the family historian's mill.

More important, however, is the need of family historians to
come to some understanding of the historical unfolding of family
sociology research and theory as a process of interaction between
family sociologists, their research and theory, and society. All three
of these elements have played interdependent roles in the development of the discipline. Similarly, family historians, their research
and theory, and the societies of which they are a part have played
and will continue to play roles in their own history.

This study of the development of American family sociology
and its evolving conceptions of the American family is the result of
my own interest in three separate areas: women's history, the
history of professions, and sociology. I became interested in the
history of American women early in my graduate career. This
interest evolved into a consideration of the family and its role in
the history of women—specifically, the degree to which the family
could adapt to better meet the needs of women. If there were limits to
the degree to which the family could be altered to meet the social
demands of women, there were limits on the freedom of women
that could not be exceeded without the abolition or circumvention
of the family. My interest, then, in the range of adaptability and
the degree of indispensability of the family became the entry point
for my study of the family and of the literature of family sociology.

Robert Wiebe's *Search for Order*[1] alerted me as a social historian
to the strategic importance of professions and professionalization
to an understanding of the development of industrial and post-

industrial society. This led me to an exploration of the literature on professionalization. I was struck by the general disregard of historians for the history of the professions. A few historians have produced important contributions to the literature, notably Daniel Calhoun in a study of the emergence of engineering as a profession, *The American Civil Engineer*, Roy Lubove with *The Professional Altruist*, which analyzed the development of social work as a profession, and most recently, Mary O. Furner in her *Advocacy and Objectivity*, for which she studied the development of academic professionalization in the social sciences in the late nineteenth and early twentieth centuries.[2]

Lubove's and Furner's works, which focused on the interrelationship between the internal development of a set of professional behaviors and mores and the external influence of the larger society, spotlighted the importance of understanding professionalization as a social as well as an intellectual process. Professionals have written histories of their own professions, but with few exceptions they are oriented to the chronological narration of the great men and ideas of their profession's past.

Sociology has been the third major interest of my graduate career. As a social historian, I soon came to realize the importance of developing a working knowledge of the theories and research discoveries of sociology. A substantial portion of my graduate career, therefore, has been devoted to developing an understanding of social theory for the purpose of providing my historical research with a more coherent and sociologically useful theoretical underpinning. I am convinced that sociologists and historians have much to gain from each other. Sociologists have long needed to provide their research and theory with an historical dimension in order to fully come to grips with the problems of social change. Historians, on the other hand, have been traditionally deficient in their understanding and application of social theory in their explanations. Common sense and insights gleaned from a close reading of relevant documents by themselves no longer suffice to explain social change in all its complexities. Happily, both historians and sociologists are becoming aware of their respective shortcomings, and in the last decade an impressive amount of interdisciplinary research has emerged, the product of both historians and sociologists.

My interests in these three areas, women and the family, the professions, and sociology, found a natural convergence in the social history of American family sociology, the topic of this study. While historians have begun to examine the social history of the social sciences, these studies have so far been confined to the nineteenth and early twentieth centuries, usually ending with the emergence of their topic of study as a distinct profession. No historian, so far as I know, has attempted to trace the history of a profession into its later and more mature stages. There are very good reasons for this, the most important of which is the superabundance of historical data. The professions are no exception to this, as most of them have voluminously recorded their past in their professional journals, position papers, professional school materials, and conference proceedings. These materials tend to increase at an exponential rate; and the closer the historian carries his research to the present, the worse the problem becomes. For the academic professions, where careers and professional prestige are tied to the publication of research findings, the problem is compounded.

Rather than limiting this study chronologically, I chose to narrow the topic to the specialty of family sociology. Even so, the research problems remained formidable. Family sociology has been a major subfield of sociology throughout the twentieth century. Through the 1940s the field was the second largest specialty within sociology. Although its position declined through the 1950s and 1960s, the field has continued to expand in terms of absolute numbers, and the volume of publication has increased correspondingly. To reduce the research data of this study to more manageable proportions, I have concentrated my analysis upon the periodical literature of family sociologists. Journal articles since the 1920s have been the major means of disseminating family sociology research, and an analysis of them reveals the focus and composition of the field as it changed over time. Journal research was augmented by an examination of the more important book-length studies of the field, as well as textbooks and edited collections.

For the period prior to 1920, I made extensive use of the textbooks of the early sociologists. Little periodical material dealing with the family appeared in the sociology journals of this time. As, the delineation of distinct specialties had not yet emerged, textbooks tended to be the major forum for the presentation of new sociological theory during these years, rather than distillations of theory and research that had become an established part of the discipline. I have not made extensive use of personal correspondence of the major figures in family sociology. Most of the history of family sociology unfolded in the years after 1920, a period when the telephone and face-to-face conversation, made possible by improvements in transportation, largely replaced written correspondence. In addition, much of what correspondence has survived is of little use. Family sociologists have not been given to much personal disclosure in their correspondence. Finally, though sociology departmental correspondence very well might prove to be of crucial importance to historians, much of it has been lost. Sociologists' realization that last month's faculty meeting minutes or departmental directives are historical data has been slow in coming, although there are signs that this attitude is changing.

As important as the primary sources of this work is the body of theory that has informed and guided the research itself. For the theoretical underpinning of this study I have relied most heavily on the writings of Stephen Toulmin, in particular the first volume of his major work, *Human Understanding*.[3] Of crucial value to any social historian of the social sciences in his concept of the development of scientific theory in terms of an "intellectual ecology." Toulmin's term is heuristically rich. To understand the development of any scientific discipline entails an understanding of not simply its theory alone but the interplay between theory and the larger intellectual environment (the scientific discipline or, in this case, the specialty) in which it operates. The term suggests that ideas, like species of animals or plants, exist within ecological niches, in which they either thrive or become extinct. The term implies a complex model of theoretical development that does more justice to the dynamics of this process than either traditional intellectual historical approaches or the sociology of knowledge.

Although the development of scientific theory can be analyzed in terms of these theories alone, this traditional intellectual history perspective does not come to grips with the relation of ideas to the discipline from which they emerge. On the other hand, to see the development of theory only as the dependent product of the social environment from which it emerges (as sociology of knowledge adherents do) fails to consider the possibility of variant or "mutant" ideas within that environment. Toulmin's concept of scientific disciplines as "rational enterprises" that create an "intellectual ecology" between theory and its adherents allows for a variable attribution of cause and effect. Theory both alters and is altered by its intellectual environment.

Though Toulmin developed this concept with the physical and natural sciences in mind, its application can be extended to the less highly developed social sciences as well. If the intellectual ecology of the physical sciences essentially remains that of its scientific community, the intellectual environment of social theory extends beyond that community to include society at large. The physical sciences provide, in this analogy, a more well-developed ecological niche, better protected from direct external social influence, than that of the social sciences; they enjoy more "closure," more protection from outside influence. In terms of this study, Toulmin's conception of "intellectual ecology" suggested the need to analyze the family sociologists, their research and theory, as an ecological system: an intellectual enterprise that interacts with the society that contains it.

Beyond this, an examination of the literature of sociology of occupations and professions helped me to understand the elements of professionalization within academic disciplines. Among the works that have proved to be particularly useful are Wilbert Moore's and Gerald W. Rosenblum's *Professions: Roles and Rules*, which provides an excellent bibliography of the literature on professionalization and a clear, concise outline of the criteria that define professions.[4] Irving Louis Horowitz's collection of essays, *Professing Sociology*, has been useful in helping me to understand the workings of professional ideology and self-definition.[5] William J. Goode's articles, "Community Within a Community: The Professions," and "Encroachment, Charlatanism, and the Emerging Profession: Psychology, Sociology, and Medicine," have proved to be very insightful.[6] His "Community Within a Community" provides an excellent discussion of the development of professional autonomy, which helped to amplify my understanding of Toulmin's concept of intellectual ecology; his second article outlines the difference between academic disciplines as professions and the classic professions such as medicine or law.

This study, then, is a social history of a sociological specialty, American family sociology, which examines family sociologists' evolving and broadening perceptions of the family in the context of the environment of their developing specialty and the transformation of American society in the century since the Civil War. This study may prove to be helpful to family sociologists in their efforts to transform their specialty into a "reflexive" discipline, one that can look to its past for insight and guidance in its preparation for the future.[7] Finally, it is hoped that this study will be a contribution to the infant field of the social history of the social sciences, and the forerunner of other such studies, which hold the promise of increasing our understanding of the role of the academic professions in the development of industrial and post-industrial society.

Many people have helped me in the process of researching and writing this study. My graduate adviser and dissertation chairman, John Lankford, has served as my intellectual guide throughout my graduate education and, more than anyone else, has been responsible for my development as a social historian. Professor Thomas Alexander's thorough reading of this work and insightful suggestions have been of great value and assistance. Professor Barbara Bank has offered useful suggestions and has encouraged my efforts in interdisciplinary research.

The manuscript staffs of the libraries of the University of Chicago, the University of North Carolina, Duke University, and the Library of Congress were very helpful in locating material in their collections. Rupert Vance, Edgar Thompson, and Leonard S. Cottrell, Jr., provided invaluable personal information about Ernest R. Groves, Charles Ellwood, and Ernest W. Burgess in the course of my conversations with them in the summer of 1974. Finally, my wife has been adviser, typist, critic, and a constant source of encouragement through the research and writing of this dissertation. To all of these individuals, I wish to express my gratitude.

NOTES

1. The full citation of this work is *The Search for Order, 1877-1920* (New York: Hill and Wang, 1967).

2. The full citations of these works are: Daniel Calhoun, *The American Engineer: Origins and Conflict* (Cambridge, Mass.: Technology Press,

Massachusetts Institute of Technology, 1960); Roy Lubove, *The Professional Altruist: The Emergence of Social Work as a Career, 1880-1930* (Cambridge, Mass.: Harvard University Press, 1965); and Mary O. Furner, *Advocacy and Objectivity: A Crisis in the Professionalization of American Social Science, 1865-1905* (Lexington, Ky.: The University Press of Kentucky, 1975).

3. *Human Understanding* (Oxford: Oxford University Press, 1972), Vol. 1: *General Introduction and Part I.* The discussion of Toulmin's ideas in the following paragraphs is most tightly defined in ibid., pp. 142-44, 165-68, 300-18, and 378-95.

4. Wilbert Ellis Moore and Gerald W. Rosenblum, *The Professions: Roles and Rules* (New York: Russell Sage Foundation, 1970).

5. *Professing Sociology: Studies in the Life Cycle of Social Science* (Chicago: Aldine Publishing Co., 1968).

6. "Community Within a Community: The Professions," *American Sociological Review* 22 (1957): 194-200 (hereinafter referred to as *ASR*); "Encroachment, Charlatanism, and the Emerging Profession: Psychology, Sociology, and Medicine," *ASR* 25 (1960): 902-14.

7. The term, "reflexive" was coined by Alvin Gouldner in his *Coming Crisis of Western Sociology* (New York: Basic Books, 1970). He used the term to refer to a "reflexive sociology," a sociology that had the ability to examine itself, to understand its own *a priori* assumptions and values and their role in building sociological theory. See pp. 481-512 for a full discussion of this concept.

CONCEPTIONS AND ATTITUDES ABOUT THE FAMILY IN NINETEENTH-CENTURY AMERICA

Ronald L. Howard

Between the Civil War and World War I, the United States was transformed from a predominantly rural and agricultural society into an urban and industrialized one. In this environment of rapid social change, the family was viewed both as an object of reform and as a topic of scholarly interest. As the object of reform, the family was perceived to be a threatened institution, one which had to be protected from pressures caused by an increasing rate of change.

Scholarly interest in the family was stimulated by the emergence of naturalism in the latter half of the nineteenth century. Based primarily upon the laws of organic evolution developed by Charles Darwin, naturalism sought to extend the application of those laws to social phenomena. The family was thought to have developed according to the laws of evolution as well. To understand this process of development shed light not only on the family but on the fundamental nature of society as well. Evolutionists dominated the development of the social sciences in nineteenth-century America and laid the foundations of present-day anthropology, economics, sociology, and history.[1] Evolutionist interest in the family developed within the emergent discipline of anthropology. It was here that the family became a major topic of interest and speculation. Their findings did not remain confined to anthropology but were incorporated into the larger analyses of the early sociologists and, to a lesser extent, into the literature of the family reformers.

The first of these studies was Sir Henry Maine's (1822-1888) *Ancient Law*, published in 1861.[2] Though this work was concerned with the development of law and legal institutions, its significance for students of the family consisted of Maine's short description of the development of legal custom, particularly with regard to the family, as a transition from "status to contract" and of his patriarchal theory of family development.

Maine's "status to contract" concept suggested that social bonds, which initially centered upon family position and joined family to family without regard to the members within it, had been transformed with the development of Western law into a new form of social bond, the contract. Unlike the bonds of status, which were predetermined by family membership, the new bonds of contract were negotiated, not between families, but between individuals.[3] This concept was borrowed and turned to the uses of the family reformers, often as a way of emphasizing the emergence of threatening "excessive individualism" to substantiate their claim that the American political system had increasingly elevated the individual at the expense of the family by recognizing and protecting individual rights without recognizing the rights of the family.[4]

The other aspect of Maine's work, his theory that the contemporary family had emerged from an unbroken chain of patriarchal forms, began the scholarly debate about the origins and evolution of the contemporary family.[5] Within a few years, Maine's theory had been challenged by John Ferguson McLennan (1827-1881) in a work entitled *Primitive Marriage*. McLennan claimed that the matrilineal patterns of descent employed by various primitive peoples around the world were survivors from an earlier age in which paternal descent was unrecognized and kinship patterns and descent were determined by maternity.[6] McLennan's challenge set the pattern of escalating scholarly research into the customs of historical and primitive peoples for each round of the debate. By the last decade of the nineteenth century, Edward Westermarck's (1862-1939) *History of Human Marriage* required three volumes of heavily footnoted text, describing the marriage customs of numerous ancient and primitive peoples to substantiate his conclusion that monogamous and patriarchal family patterns were everywhere the rule.[7]

The early sociologists after Comte, Herbert Spencer (1820-1903),

Lester Frank Ward (1841-1913), Franklin Henry Giddings (1855-1931), and William Graham Sumner (1840-1910), employed the findings of the anthropologists in their own writings and interpreted these findings in light of their broader analyses of the origins and development of society.[8] Herbert Spencer was a major proponent of a theory of family evolution. His analysis did not spell out the duties and obligations of the family and its members to each other, but his general conception was of an evolution away from ascribed social duties and obligations toward societies characterized by voluntary, contractual relationships. This position led Spencer to sanction the institution of divorce. Marriage, along with other social relationships, was destined to become a voluntary, contractual relationship, held together not by legal restrictions, but by the bonds of affection and sentiment. Spencer predicted that society would eventually reject the continued imposition of legal and social sanctions to preserve a marriage within which the bonds of affection and sentiment had died. He tried to temper his radical view by predicting that though society would come to accept divorce, the need for it would simultaneously abate, as people came to take more care in marrying.[9]

Spencer used child and female welfare as a means of determining the progress of the family to higher forms.[10] The earliest forms were accompanied, in his belief, by a primitive and barbaric status for women and children, one that steadily improved with the continuing development of the family.[11] Spencer saw the transition from a patriarchally dominated family to a situation of more equitable co-partnership as a progressive trend. His stance in relation to women's rights was moderate, however; and he believed that women, given the complete freedom to decide their own destiny, would choose to remain within the home.[12]

The family of the future, Spencer believed, would be judged by the addition of a third criterion: its ability to care for the aged. As the monogamous family provided the highest concentration of parental attention to the child, the children of such families would be those most likely to take upon themselves the care of aged parents as well as the care of their own children. Hence, it was within the vested interest of the parent to care for his children, as such care would very likely be returned.[13]

Lester Frank Ward in his work, *Dynamic Sociology*, also used the

status and position of women as a gauge of family evolution,
though he came to different conclusions than did Spencer. He saw
that the inauguration of human family life had been accompanied
by a decline in the status of women to a position of inferiority to
men which was only beginning to reverse itself.[14] The emergence of
woman's rights Ward saw as a sign of the return of woman to her
rightful place, if not of superiority, at least of equality. Ward en-
visioned life in a society that enjoyed sexual equality to the extent
that both sexes would wear similar clothes.[15] Though he never
explicitly mentioned it, his general conception clearly implied a
sharing of all roles between the sexes, including that of caring for
children. He saw nothing immutable in the traditional roles of the
sexes. The purpose of sociology for Ward was not to imitate nature,
but to improve upon it.[16]

Franklin Henry Giddings in his first major work, *Principles of
Sociology*, gave scant attention to the family. To the extent that
he did, he shared Spencer's conceptions about the evolution of the
family. He saw the replacement of the religious proprietary family
based upon ascribed position and status by the romantic family,
bound together by ties of affection and sentiment, an arrangement
that had remained stable as long as women remained economically
dependent and divorce was difficult. With the emergence of woman's
rights and the liberalization of divorce, this family form had
become unstable.[17] He believed that the eventual stable family form
would be the ethical family, bound together by sentiment composed
of passion, admiration and respect, physical fitness, the ability to
maintain a pleasant home, and a high sense of the duty and privilege
of transmitting these qualities to their children.[18]

Giddings saw, with Maine, that society had become unstable
through an excessive assertion of individual rights. He saw the cure
in the ascendance of a socially enlightened rationality that would
temper individual choices with a sense of social responsibility. With
Spencer, Giddings believed that alternative forms of family life,
either free love or marriage coupled with easy divorce, would fail to
replicate themselves. Such marriages would most likely be childless
and would concede the field to the ethical family, which would be
capable of reproducing itself.[19]

William Graham Sumner viewed the family as the evolutionary

result of the accretion of sexual customs and mores.[20] While a believer in the evolutionary development of social institutions, he saw nothing natural in any particular arrangement of parents and children. Matrimonial patterns were conventional, the result of custom and tradition.[21] Though conceding an evolutionary sequence to the development of marriage institutions, Sumner did not subscribe to a concept of moral evolution that accompanied these forms; no single form of familial arrangement in and of itself was superior to another. All demanded consistency to the mores associated with them, and Sumner saw no reason to believe that morality was any more or less restrictive with one system than another.[22] Though he concluded that monogamy was the form of marriage most conducive to human happiness, Sumner did not believe that this was uniformly or invariably so.[23]

Sumner took a dispassionate, descriptive view toward the institutions of the family and marriage. Although he conceded that the recent development of civilization had been accompanied by a loss of family functions, he saw its salvation in parents who were able to adapt to changing times. He realized that the family as a source of conservative traditionalism was passing away, but he saw nothing in this that gave cause for alarm.[24] While he believed that confining divorce to the biblical grounds for adultery was far too restrictive, he was not an advocate of unrestricted divorce. He believed unrestricted divorce would reduce marriage to a nullity and provide no incentive for meeting the responsibilities of married life.[25] His attitude toward woman's rights was equally noncommittal. Noting the general dependency of women, Sumner observed that, traditionally, women needed marriage more than men. Physiology, rather than social custom, ultimately explained the unequal sexual burdens of childbirth and nurture ascribed to the women.[26] Events of the latter half of the nineteenth century had come to change this, and it was becoming possible for women to contemplate careers outside the family circle. As a result, modern society would evolve away from an acceptance of marriage as the universal state for all its adult members.[27]

These four sociologists, Spencer, Ward, Giddings, and Sumner, shared a common evolutionist perspective of the origins and development of the family as an institution but, influenced by personal attitudes, derived different conclusions from it. These personal differences were overshadowed by a common faith in the adaptability of the family as an institution to new social conditions. This faith was not shared by the reformers, who saw the family as a threatened institution. The family reformers encompassed a wide variety of people—clergymen, legal scholars, social reformers, and charity workers. The family reformers can be divided into two types: moral reformers, who concentrated their attention on moral evils they believed threatened the family, and environmental reformers, who tended to see the threats to the family in terms of the conditions of industrializing American society.

For the moral reformers, the greatest threat by far to family survival was divorce. As a topic of debate, it dominated the literature of the family in the nineteenth century. Divorce was a complex subject, not easily separated from other issues. The unfolding debate over the topic involved a large number of issues, among them women's rights and the relationship between individual rights and family obligations. The nature of this debate and its progress has been discussed at length elsewhere and will not be repeated here.[28] Instead, our attention will be directed to what the literature of the family tells us about the family itself, its functions, the relationships it had with other institutions of society, and the factors that helped or hindered it as an institution. This literature nowhere provides a totally inclusive portrait. Preoccupied with the elements they saw threatening the family, none of the family reformers provided more than a partial view of the institution and its functions. What follows is a composite of views of the family as it appeared in this scattered literature.[29]

The family was believed to be the fundamental unit of society. Without the family, society could not survive, and its health could be gauged by the condition of family life within it. The family was seen to be society in miniature, a little commonwealth, whose network of interrelationships both suggested and anticipated the relationships of society at large. The family was believed to be the first social institution, from which all other social institutions subsequently developed.[30]

The family was viewed as the primary means of socialization and was believed to have no equal for this purpose.[31] For the child to learn the rules of family life, its responsibilities and obligations, was to effectively prepare for membership in society at large. The importance of the family for the socialization of the young was based upon the observation that children were particularly susceptible to the influence of others, as they were given to intense observation and imitation of the people around them.[32] This idea was particularly important in the religious literature. The family was an indispensable aid to the process of religious education. Piety began in the home, and was best learned while young from parental instruction and example.[33]

Inherent in the susceptibility of children to outside influence was their vulnerability to it as well. Sensitive to the behavior of others, children were believed to lack the ability to discriminate between acceptable and unacceptable forms of behavior. This belief reinforced the ethical responsibility of parents; what a child became was a reflection of the examples the parents set.[34] This concept served as the central argument of many moral reformers, particularly Anthony Comstock. Whatever evils noxious and vile literature contained, it operated with redoubled force upon the impressions and sensibilities of the young.[35] For Charles Loring Brace, the impressionable character of children was both a cause for alarm and a cause for hope. Left to the malignant influence of the street, the saloon, and the criminal, the orphaned, neglected, or abandoned child was certain to become a member of the "dangerous classes" of urban America. Placed within the benign environment of a farm family or, failing this, within an institution modelled as closely after the family as possible, the same child would become a useful member of society.[36]

Particularly important for the children, the positive values of family life extended to the parents as well. For the women, it provided the personal fulfillment of motherhood. For both parents, family life was believed to be the source of continuing education and development of character. The quickening of parental love stimulated the development of the qualities of self-sacrifice, patience, and concern for others. The adult who remained outside the confines of matrimony and family life was believed to be an incomplete person, given to selfishness and social irresponsibility.[37]

For philanthropists and charity workers concerned with the

problems of orphaned or abandoned homeless children, experience indicated that the family was essential to infant survival. By the early 1870s charity organizations had gathered enough evidence to show that even the best of foundling homes meant death sentences for most of their charges.[38] Though the precise element that family life provided for infant survival had not been discovered, the empirical relationship had; infants left to foundling homes died in appallingly high numbers. The smaller the institutional setting, and the closer its conditions approached those of family life, the lower the mortality rate. Finally, infants boarded out to families enjoyed a mortality rate similar to that of the infant population at large.[39]

The perspective of the family as a threatened social institution provided a prescriptive analysis of the conditions that promoted or hindered the family.[40] Within this perspective, the elements which threatened the family were viewed as intruders—disturbers of the normal conditions of family life that supposedly had existed before the emergence of these threats. The most common prescriptive condition for healthy family life was a rural environment. The city was believed to be a destroyer of families and the locus for most of the evils that threatened the family.[41]

The ideal rural family was patriarchal, organized under the authority of the father. It was a self-contained economic and political unit, earning its living from farming, an occupation that fostered cooperation among all the members of the family and provided each of them with a sense of self-worth, for all had an important part to play in the common good.[42]

A second beneficial quality attributed to family life in the country was its healthfulness. The child's need for strenuous activity was far more easily met in the country than in the city. Such a life promoted not only the physical health of the child, but a sense of inventiveness and independence as well. The home-grown amusements of the country child were held up in favorable comparison to the prepared or commercial amusements upon which the city child was supposedly dependent.[43] Although the concepts of mental health were in their infancy in the nineteenth century, the countryside, with its natural lifestyle, was seen to bear some relation to the mental health of its inhabitants. In this literature naturalness was equated with the avoidance of extremes; country life provided a balance that city life could not.[44]

Closely tied to the question of health was the condition of housing. It was believed that family life was carried on best in the detached, single-family dwelling typical of life in the countryside; it was stunted or destroyed altogether in the conditions of tenement life in the cities.[45] Home ownership was believed to be a factor that promoted family stability. It encouraged the newly married couple to raise a family and settle down. It promoted a sense of social responsibility by creating a stake in society for the home owner and his family that tenement or boarding house living could not provide.[46]

Taken together, the family reform literature of the nineteenth century provided a composite picture of the ideal family as a patriarchal rural family, tied to tradition, the primary vehicle of socialization. It was a static picture, however, one which stood in opposition to the character of industrializing American society of the latter half of the nineteenth century.

The early charity workers shared these views of the family with the moral reformers and those environmental reformers whose efforts did not bring them into actual charity work. Their perspective shifted, however, as a result of direct contact with the destitute and dependent. During the 1880s, they began to abandon their early beliefs about the family in exchange for a working pragmatism, which, while less conceptually integrated, better served their needs.

Many of the early charity workers were conservative in their attitudes toward the poor. They believed poverty to be an individual problem rather than the result of societal failure, for which individual treatment rather than general social reform was the remedy. Instead of material relief, then, advice and information would be given to help the poor help themselves.[47]

The depression of 1873 led to a sharp increase in the number of destitute families and in the number of philanthropic societies dispensing material relief to the poor. Many charity workers, believing that indiscriminant material relief was a cause of the increase in the numbers of the poor, viewed the growth of these societies with alarm.[48] To stem the growth in the numbers of the poor, they believed, charity work would have to be controlled and organized. This belief led to the establishment of charity organization societies.

The lasting significance of the charity organization societies lay in their methods rather than the attitudes of the charity organizers themselves. Charity organization societies did dispense some material aid, but their main functions were to provide information and advice to the poor and to serve as referral agencies for charitable organizations already in existence. To carry out these tasks, charity organization societies recruited large numbers of "friendly visitors." These volunteers periodically called on the needy to determine, through observation and interrogation, the actual state and needs of the families requesting aid.[49] This information was recorded in case records, initially to keep track of families receiving material aid in order to prevent them from obtaining illegitimate aid from several competing charitable societies, but increasingly to serve functions similar to medical case records. They recorded the diagnosis of the needy family's problems, the treatment prescribed, and the results achieved.[50] These case records provided an empirical basis for the testing and development of concepts and methods of charitable aid. More and more, the efficacy of any given reform proposal was not taken at face value. Charity workers became increasingly concerned with the practical necessity of determining what worked, when measured in statistical terms, rather than subscribing to what logically followed from a given moral position. In the course of this transition, charity workers laid down some of the traditions of empirical research that have remained in both American sociology and social work since.

In general, the family reformers held the family to be more than a mere secular institution, whose bonds were sanctioned not only by civil authority but by religious law. Gradually, the charity workers abandoned the concept that the natural family invariably enjoyed ethical and religious approval. Natural parentage was no guarantee of the blessings of family life, and charity workers came to see it as their duty to remove children from their natural but negligent or criminal parents and place them in foster homes with people who would supply the care and attention these children did not receive from their natural parents.[51] For the charity worker, the essential quality of family life was the element of care and concern it provided the children, rather than the ties of kinship. This concept was backed by the legal maxim that society had a right to protect itself; to leave the child in a home environment where it was acculturated to the life of the criminal or the social indigent was a threat to society.[52]

The effects of day-to-day child-saving inevitably shifted the perspective of the charity workers. The realities of their problems found no immediate solutions in the stock of moral sentiments that had initially motivated them, and they were increasingly confronted with situations requiring individual, pragmatic assessment rather than the simple application of a moral maxim. For example, they were often faced with the problems of abandoned mothers and their children, which required perennial reassessments of the essentials of adequate family life. Was it right to remove the child from the widowed or abandoned wife, who was forced to leave the children to their own devices much of the time, in order to work and keep together the family her departed husband left behind? No clear-cut solution presented itself, beyond trying to judge each case upon its merits, including the character of the mother, and trying to act upon the principle that one concerned parent was better than none.[53]

The charity worker lauded the joys and virtues of family life as much as the moral reformer; but the family itself came to be seen as a variable quality, not only with regard to parents but with regard to the environmental conditions of family life as well.

More and more, good family life was seen to be the product of an adequate environment. By the 1880s the charity workers began to realize that bad housing and overcrowding were as visibly destructive of family life as negligent or criminal parents.[54] Consistent in their conservatism, they did not at first try to deal with the problem of poor housing directly through housing legislation or the promotion of philanthropic housing projects. Instead, they directed their attention to providing a proper environment for the child outside the household through the agency of the kindergarten. The hope was to provide moral education through play at an age when the child had not yet become hardened to his environment and indifferent to outside suggestion.[55] By 1888, Felix Adler (1851-1933), a German-born educational reformer, suggested that manual training could provide the benefits in building the character of older children that kindergarten provided for younger children.[56] Though James McKeen Cattell (1860-1944) would argue in 1909 that educational institutions helped to undermine the family, many charity workers of the 1880s believed that educational institutions were an excellent means of overcoming the deficiencies of poor home environments.[57]

Charity workers were awakening to the realization that much

more must be known about the family before its problems could be dealt with effectively. In 1884, Frederick H. Wines (1838-1912), president of the National Conference of Charities and Correction, called upon charity workers to organize and become scientific. He asked that they abandon a priori conceptions, establish theories based upon scientific collection of social facts, and employ methods that proved themselves by results.[58] He went on to suggest that social reform could not be effective without an understanding "of the subtle connection which exists between the parts of the social organism, the logical interdependence of their relations, and the immensity of the possible consequences which may follow any injudicious interference."[59] The moral sentiments behind social reform were no longer sufficient. Moral sentiment would have to be tempered and augmented by social knowledge; an understanding of social anatomy and social pathology would have to precede the mastery of social therapeutics.[60]

For most of the second half of the nineteenth century, the relationship between the family reformers and the evolutionists remained congenial. On the one hand, the literature of the family reformers remained beneath academic interest and scrutiny. On the other, the family reformers generally accepted the credentials of the academic and scholarly students of the family at face value and did not presume to be critical of their activities. In addition, both of these groups shared complementary conceptions of the contemporary family. If the reformers saw the family as the cornerstone of society, most of the scholarly students assumed that the contemporary monogamous family was the end of the chain of development and the highest expression of family organization.[61] Even the proponents of the more exotic scholarly views, such as those who suggested that matriarchal or polygamous family patterns played an important role in the development of the contemporary family, did not imply that such forms were appropiate in present-day society. Moreover, the intellectual debate among the evolutionists became less relevant to the reformers as it increasingly focused on the deeper and more speculative recesses of the family's past and its more exotic and less-known variants among contemporary peoples.[62]

The views of the early sociologists eventually came into conflict with the moral reformers. The actual clash between these two groups did not emerge, however, until the end of the century, partly because the moral reformers were unaware of most of the early sociologists, aside from Spencer, and partly through the efforts of Samuel Warren Dike (1839-1913). Dike was acknowledged by many to be the preeminent family expert in the United States by the end of the 1880s and was the principal officer of the major divorce reform organization of the nineteenth century, the National Divorce Reform League. Retaining the traditional attitudes and sentiments toward the family characteristic of the moral reformers, Dike tried to employ the theories of sociology and methods of statistics to further their cause. A Congregationalist minister, Dike rose to prominence in the cause of divorce reform in 1881 with a speech he delivered in Boston.[63] The speech prompted some of Boston's more influential moral reformers to encourage Dike to consider a career in divorce reform, forming the New England Divorce Reform League (later renamed the National Divorce Reform League) for this purpose and collecting a subscription for Dike's salary.[64]

As corresponding secretary for the Divorce Reform League, Dike delivered speeches for the cause and managed the publications and correspondence of the League, but not in the expected manner. Although his Boston speech had dwelt at great length on the moral evils of lax divorce laws, the speech closed on a note calling for further study and education to better understand the divorce problem. Three years later, an article by Dike in the *Princeton Review* illustrated how far from traditional moral rhetoric he had moved. Though the article discussed the divorce problem briefly in the opening paragraphs, the bulk of the article expanded into a discussion of the development of individualism in England and the United States and the effects of this development on family, economic, and political institutions.[65] The following year, in a similar article in the *Homiletic Review*, Dike openly stated that the divorce problem in the United States could not be understood without a full knowledge of the historical development of the family and its relation with other social institutions.[66] Divorce, for Dike, was not a problem that could be simply understood or solved; it was closely related and connected with many of the other problems facing the family, such as intemperance, pauperism, and crime. By the mid-

1880s, Dike had moved from being simply a divorce reform advocate to a promoter of the new science of sociology.

His interest in sociology was matched by his enthusiasm for the gathering of social statistics, which he believed vital to any understanding of social problems; and it was in the area of social statistics that he achieved his greatest success. Following four years of almost single-handed advocacy, Dike managed to persuade Congress to appropriate money for a study of marriage and divorce. This study, *A Report on Marriage and Divorce 1867-1887*, published in 1889, was one of the major collections of social statistics compiled in the nineteenth century.[67] In the years immediately following the publication of the report, Dike rose to the height of his influence.[68] Although his religious beliefs prevented him from adopting the comparatively dispassionate perspective that the early sociologists maintained toward the family, he remained a strong advocate for the new science and a continuous promoter of the gathering of social statistics.

Dike's authority both as the leader of the major divorce reform organization and as the preeminent family expert of the late nineteenth century probably explained his ability to direct his League toward goals that many of his supporters were suspicious of and eventually opposed. Dike personally transformed the Divorce Reform League from a partisan lobby devoted to enacting restrictive divorce laws into an organization that promoted the gathering of social statistics and the new science of sociology. He served as its sole spokesman, and his annual reports had as their purpose the education of his supporters rather than the inflammation of their moral repugnance of divorce. The success of his efforts can be gauged by the financial statistics of the League, which were included in the *Annual Reports*. Dike's income was totally derived from his subscribers, and from 1888 through 1902 the annual subscription rate exceeded $2,000, sufficient to meet his annual salary of $1,500 and pay the expenses of the organization with little or no deficit. After this period, both the number of his subscribers and the League's income steadily declined until, by the end of the first decade of the twentieth century, they stood at about half the peak year of 1890, when the League's income totalled just under $3,000.

By 1910, Dike no longer had the authority to restrain his supporters from openly attacking sociology as an opponent to divorce restriction. His attempts to use his organization as a bridge between moral reformers and the new science of sociology ended in failure, but it is a testament to his skill and diplomacy that he succeeded as long as he did.

In 1887, the year the first American textbook on the family was published, much of this discontent remained in the future. This book, *The Family*, by Charles Franklin Thwing (1853-1937) and his wife, Carrie F. Butler Thwing (1855-1898), is illustrative of both aspects of nineteenth-century interest in the family.[69] While the authors were representatives of the moral reformers of the family, they devoted ninety pages of their 213-page text to the history of the family and a discussion of the theories of the scholarly students of the family. The remainder of their book involved a prescriptive analysis of the contemporary family in the light of Christian doctrine and concluded with an analysis of the role of the family as a social institution in the larger society and a discussion of the various threats facing the contemporary family.

The Thwings believed that the family was a conservative institution that protected society from the radical excesses of unrestrained individualism. They shared a basic fear of individual freedom, believing that the individual was selfish and depraved. The failure to recognize this fact explained the failure of such utopian socialist experiments in communal living as Oneida and predisposed the Thwings to take a dim view of any form of communalistic social organization.[70] Children provided the essential means of restraining the unbridled impulses of individual desire, for it was the common love of parents for their children and their concern for their children's welfare that caused parents to restrain their bickering and settle their individual differences.[71] Parental love engendered the desire to meet familial and social responsibilities; individual self-interest led to a contempt for social authority.

The Thwings' fear of the individual caused them to take an ambivalent stance toward the question of women's rights. They opposed many of the traditional legal prerogatives the husband exerted over the wife, particularly over the disposition of family property and authority over the children. Indeed, the Thwings went so far as to question whether the Bible in fact sanctioned the subordination of women to men and strongly advocated the sharing of family authority equally between husband and wife.[72] On the other hand, they believed that the woman's place was in the home and expressed concern that the growing movement for women's rights was being advanced without an equal concern for the parallel advancement of women's responsibilities.[73] In particular, they regarded the women's rights movement as one of the causes for the rising divorce rate, which they viewed as a social evil and threat to the family.[74]

The Thwings focused upon divorce as the major evil threatening the contemporary family.[75] They devoted less attention to environmental evils threatening the family, though they believed that the growth of urban life promoted the evils of excessive individualism. Believers in the rural ideal, they yet took a passive attitude toward the growth of cities and optimistically believed that the flow of the population to the cities at some future date would reverse itself and the problems of city life would thus decline.[76]

The Thwings' work serves as the best single representative of the entire field of interest in the family in the second half of the nineteenth century, combining an ethical concern for the continued safety of the family with a speculative, scholarly interest in its origins and historical development. At its core, the field rested upon a network of beliefs about the family so firmly entrenched that the degree to which they conformed to reality remained unquestioned.[77]

Yet, by 1887, elements of change were already in existence that would in the next three decades transform the field of interest in the family from moral debate and speculative scholarship to a scientific enterprise committed to gathering empirical evidence about its nature. Charity workers and moral reformers like Samuel Dike found themselves advocates of the new science of sociology, but the sociology of that time, speculative and based upon evolutionary concepts, did not meet their needs. After 1890 a new approach to sociological inquiry was developed that led in that decade to a convergence between the fields of sociology and social work.

NOTES

1. An excellent discussion of naturalism in American thought can be found in Stow Person's *American Minds: A History of Ideas* (New York: Henry Holt and Company, 1958), pp. 217-345.

2. *Ancient Law: Its Connection with the Early History of Society and Its Relation to Modern Ideas*, introduction and notes, Sir Fredrick Pollock, 4th American edition from the 10th London edition (New York: Holt [1885].

3. Ibid., pp. 163-65.

4. The concept of "excessive individualism" as a natural consequence of the shift to contract relationships, with its attendant legal recognition of individual rights while not recognizing family rights, was widespread and often accompanied attacks upon the liberalization of divorce. See Charles Franklin Thwing and Carrie F. Butler Thwing, *The Family: An Historical and Social Study* (Boston: Lee and Shepard, 1887), pp. 102-9. Noah Davis equated the primacy of individualism over the interest of society with barbarism in his article, "Marriage and Divorce," *North American Review* 139 (July 1884): 34. Probably the most extensive and recurrent expositor of the theme of excessive individualism was Samuel W. Dike. See, for example, his article, "Some Aspects of the Divorce Question," *Princeton Review* 60 (March 1884): 169-90.

5. Maine's exposition of his patriarchal theory is diffuse and is never explicitly stated as such. It is most clearly present in his chapter, *Primitive Society and Ancient Law*," *Ancient Law*, pp. 109-65.

6. See, in particular, Chapter 8, "Ancient Systems of Kinship and Their Influence on the Structure of Primitive Groups," (New York: Macmillan, 1886 ed.), pp. 83-106.

7. Edward A. Westermarck, *History of Human Marriage*, 3 vols. (London: Macmillan and Co., 1894-1901).

8. For the purpose of this chapter, the early sociologists included those who were active before the University of Chicago's Department of Social Science and Anthropology became active in 1892 under the direction of Albion Small. Franklin Henry Giddings barely fits this criterion, having been appointed as a lecturer in sociology at Columbia in 1891. His major work, *The Principles of Sociology*, appeared five years later. Lester Frank Ward's *Dynamic Sociology*, published in 1884, was the first major American work in sociology. Herbert Spencer, both as a philosopher and sociologist, was popular and widely known in the United States from the early 1870s. An important part of his theory of family evolution appeared in an article entitled "On Evolution of the Family," in *Popular Science Monthly* 9

(1877): 129-42. He was influential before the 1890s, if not in his writings, certainly through his lectures, which were later distilled into his essays. Albert Galloway Kaller, in his *Reminiscences (Mainly Personal) of William Graham Sumner* (New Haven: Yale University Press, 1933), pointed out that of his own mid-1890s class of 275 students, just under two hundred attended Sumner's lecture course at Yale. By then, Sumner had already achieved the reputation of being something of an institution there (pp. 3, 8). Certainly, Sumner was widely known as an economist and social philosopher by that time. His reticence in publishing the material that later came to comprise his essays and his monumental work, *Folkways*, may well have stemmed from his moral prudery. Keller's portrait of Sumner depicts a model gentleman of Victorian mores, one who carefully excised all referents of sexual customs from his lectures during the time a young lady sat in the course, only to insert the deleted material during a later lecture from which the lady was absent (pp. 51-52). Finally, Sumner himself, in his introduction to *Folkways: A Study of the Sociological Importance of Usage, Manners, Customs, Mores, and Morals* (Boston: Ginn and Company, The Athenaeum Press, 1906), notes that the material for this book, begun in 1899, was gathered from lectures delivered over the previous decade and a half (p. iii).

9. *Principles of Sociology*, 3 vols., 3rd ed. (New York: D. Appleton and Company, 1899) 1: 765-66.

10. Ibid., 1: 734-35, 755.

11. Ibid., 1: 756.

12. Ibid., 1: 769.

13. Ibid., 1: 772.

14. The full title of this work is *Dynamic Sociology or Applied Social Science as Based upon Statistical Sociology and the Less Complex Sciences*, 2 vols., 2nd ed. (D. Appleton and Company, 1897), 1: 613-15.

15. Ibid., 1: 646-54.

16. Ibid., 1: 662.

17. *The Principles of Sociology: An Analysis of the Phenomena of Association and of Social Organization* (New York and London: Macmillan and Co., 1896), pp. 333-35, 414-15.

18. Ibid., pp. 352-53.

19. Ibid., pp. 415-16. See also Spencer, *Principles of Sociology*, 1: 718-24, 767.

20. *Folkways*, pp. 345-46.

21. Ibid., pp. 346-47.

22. Ibid., p. 353. Sumner used the criterion of "appropriateness"; some

matrimonial forms were more appropriate to a given society than were others (p. 350-52).
23. Ibid., p. 377.
24. "The Family and Social Change," *Essays of William Graham Sumner*, ed. by Albert Galloway Keller and Maurice R. Davie, 2 vols. (New Haven: Yale University Press, 1934), 1: 254.
25. "Modern Marriage," ibid., 1: 280. Sumner regarded divorce as inevitable and found no example of successful absolute prohibition of divorce. See *Folkways*, pp. 380-81.
26. *Folkways*, p. 362.
27. "Modern Marriage," 1: 283-84.
28. The most complete account of the debate over divorce in the late nineteenth and early twentieth centuries can be found in William L. O'Neill's *Divorce in the Progressive Era* (New Haven, Conn.: Yale University Press, 1967). For a shorter account, see the same author's article with the same title in *American Quarterly* 17 (1965): 203-17. Also useful is Nelson Manfred Blake's *Road to Reno: A History of Divorce in the United States* (New York: Macmillan, 1962), particularly chapters 7-10.
29. The composite picture of the family presented in this chapter is, I believe, a fair representation of the views on the family in the literature which I examined. It is based upon a study of all the articles listed in Poole's *Index to Periodical Literature, 1801-1906*, 6 vols. (New York: Houghton Mifflin, 1882-1908; reprint ed., Gloucester, Mass.: Peter Smith, 1938), under the heading, "Family." In addition, I made a systematic canvass of all issues of the following journals for the time periods indicated of all articles about the family or related subjects, such as divorce, women's rights, children, and marriage: *North American Review* (1850-1920), *Scribner's Monthly-Century Magazine* (1870-1910), and *The Nation* (1865-1920). Three theological journals were also included: *Andover Review* (1884-1893), *Biblioteca Sacra* (1850-1920), and *Methodist Review* (1850-1920). These journals were selected with the aid of Frank Luther Mott's *American Magazines*, 5 vols. (vol. 1, New York: 1938-1968), on criteria of quality and influence. All were influential, high-quality journals, and all took some notice of problems of the family. None represented extreme radical or reactionary viewpoints. *Scribner's Monthly-Century Magazine* and *Methodist Review* maintained the most consistently conservative and traditionalist viewpoints on the family and other related social issues. The other journals generally fell into a moderately conservative position on family issues, although *North American Review* would occasionally present a wide spectrum of viewpoints on social issues such as divorce. Finally, this canvass included all the issues of the *Journal of Social Science* (1869-1909).

30. All these conceptions about the family contained in this paragraph have a long history and were embodied in seventeenth-century Puritan conceptions of the family. An excellent discussion of Puritan family conceptions can be found in Edmund S. Morgan's *Puritan Family: Religion and Domestic Relations in Seventeenth-Century New England*, new ed., rev. and enl. (New York: Harper and Row, Torchbook, 1966), particularly the essay, "The Family in the Social Order" (pp. 133-60). In the nineteenth-century literature the concept that the family was the first social institution was substantiated by the book of Genesis in the Bible, according to M. Valentine. The creation of Eve to alleviate Adam's loneliness led to the formation of the first family. See his article, "The Relation of the Family to the Church," *Evangelical Review* 10 (1859): 361. The family as a miniature state, containing within it the model of the state at large, was developed by N. Green in his "Great Laboratory of Society—the Family," *Cumberland Presbyterian Quarterly Review* 4 (1883): 97-98, and by M. H. Buckham in his article, "The Relation of the Family to the State," *International Review* 13 (1882): 56. James Cardinal Gibbons, in his article, "Is Divorce Wrong?" *North American Review* 149 (1889): 30-41, developed a correlation between the rise of divorce as a destroyer of the family and the decline of civilization. Noah Davis elaborated upon this conception of the family as the fundamental social institution. Without it, society was not possible. See his article, "Marriage and Divorce," *North American Review* 139 (1884): 30. Theodore D. Woolsey presented a similar view in his article, "The Moral Statistics of the United States," *Journal of Social Science* 13 (1881): 132. This conception of the family as the fundamental social institution, upon whose well-being the continued existence of society depends, has been durable and periodically reappears in the family literature, the most recent major example being Carle C. Zimmerman's *Family of Tomorrow* (New York: Harper and Brothers, 1949).

31. This theme was often brought out in the literature of early social work, usually in connection with a discussion of the evils of "Institutionalization," which was equated with the destruction of spontaneity and individuality, lack of initiative, and stunted personality development as a result of lack of love and attention. See W. F. Letchworth's "Report on Dependent and Delinquent Children," [*National*] *Conference of Charities [and Correction]* 4 (1877): 60-80 (hereinafter cited as *NCCC*); Henry W. Lord, "Dependent and Delinquent Children, with Especial Reference to Girls," *NCCC* 5 (1878): 168-74; Anna Hallowell, "The Care and Saving of Neglected Children," *Journal of Social Science* 12 (1880): 117-24.

32. In comparison to other social science disciplines, the field of child study has a long history as an empirical enterprise. The tradition of parents

keeping diaries on the behavior of their children extends to before the beginning of the nineteenth century. For brief accounts of this development, see Florence Manteer's *Child Behavior* (Boston: R. G. Badger, 1918) pp. 13-21, and Charles W. Waddle's *Introduction to Child Psychology* (New York: Houghton Mifflin, 1918) pp. 16-20. While the history of child study as an empirical science in America begins with G. Stanley Hall's study of Boston children, "The Content of Children's Minds," *Princeton Review* 11 (1883): 249-72, Bernard W. Wishy, in his work, *The Child and the Republic: The Dawn of Modern Child Nurture* (Philadelphia: University of Pennsylvania Press, 1968), pointed out that Jacob Abbott, in his work *Gentle Measures in the Management and Training of the Young* (New York: Harper, 1871), had made the crucial observation that children are influenced more by what parents do than what they say, over a decade earlier (p. 97). While this does not dispell the possibility that many parents in the nineteenth century still raised their children under the old Puritan assumption that they were possessed of an innately wicked nature (see Morgan, *Puritan Family*, pp. 93-95), the modern idea that children's characters and personalities are developed through the imitation of their parents' behavior is apparently older than might initially be supposed.

33. This idea is central to J. W. Santee's criticism of the Sunday School movement. Religious education and salvation of the child's soul was the responsibility of the family and could not be delegated to an outside organization, even the Sunday School. See his article, "The Sunday School in Its Relation to the Church," *Reformed Church Review* 20 (July 1873): 391-421. Also see Tryon Edwards' article, "Family Training in the Christian Church," *Catholic Presbyterian* 3 (1880): 18-19.

34. This idea was developed in the opening pages of Comstock's book, *Traps for the Young* (New York: Funk and Wagnalls, 1883; reprint ed., edited by Robert Bremmer, Cambridge: Harvard University Press, Belknap Press, 1967), p. 9. Also see Green, "Great Laboratory," p. 99, and "The Family," in William D. P. Bliss, ed., *Encyclopedia of Social Reform* (New York: Funk and Wagnalls, 1897), p. 591.

35. Comstock, *Traps for the Young*, pp. 8-9.

36. *The Dangerous Classes of New York* (New York: Wynkoop and Hallenbeck, 1872), pp. 28-31, 115-17, 225, and 399-403. Also see Brace's article, "The Best Method of Founding Children's Charities in Towns and Villages," *NCCC* 7 (1880): 228-29.

37. These ideas are old and widespread throughout the literature. They formed a part of Puritan doctrine; see Morgan, *Puritan Family*, pp. 142-46. Also see Edward Trumbill Hooker, "The Family and the Church," *Biblioteca Sacra* 43 (July 1886): 486-506; Davis, "Marriage and Divorce," pp.

30-41; Edward McPherson, "The Family in Its Relation to the State," *Evangelical Review* 11 (1860): 43-61; and Buckham, "Relation of Family to State," p. 54.

38. See chapter 24, "What Shall Be Done with Foundlings?" in Brace, *Dangerous Classes*, pp. 405-17. In the course of this chapter, which cites numerous infant mortality statistics, Brace pointed out that the concept of "placing out" foundlings was already a centuries-old tradition in France.

39. For the fullest explication of this empirical relationship, see F. B. Sanborn's article, "The Treatment of Children in Institutions," *NCCC* 9 (1882), pp. 204-7. Sanborn suspected some kind of infection of undetermined origin was introduced into the wards where infants were kept and infected the healthy infants from sick ones. Sanborn and his staff resorted to placing babies in smaller and smaller quarters, until finally there were no more than four to a room. Each reorganization effectively lowered the mortality statistics. In all probability, each of these reorganizations was accompanied by an increase in the attention each infant received. This was the vital element. This conclusion is reinforced by Sanborn's observation that sickly infants removed from the institutions and placed in the care of individual wet nurses living outside the city limits (of Boston) generally improved.

40. This is not to be taken to mean that no material appeared on the family alone, but that in comparison with the literature which discussed the family in relation to the threats it faced, such material was scanty. Those articles which discussed the family with little or no regard to the threats it faced appeared in religious journals. See Hooker, "Family and Church," pp. 486-506; Edwards, "Family Training," pp. 17-24; Valentine, "Relation of Family to Church," pp. 360-80; [Phillip] Schaff, "The Influence of Christianity on the Family," *Mercerberg Quarterly Review* 5 (1853): pp. 473-91; and McPherson, "Family's Relation to State," pp. 43-61.

41. An extensive development of the rural ideal of family life can be found in Henry Ling Taylor's "American Childhood from a Medical Standpoint," *Journal of Social Science* 30 (1892): 44-55. Here virtually all the scattered conceptions of the value of rural life can be found that are contained in the literature examined in this chapter. See also, Charles D. Kellogg's "Child Life in City and Country," *Journal of Social Science* 21 (1886): 207-23.

42. The idea of family social and economic independence being a positive good is often implied in the view that the dependent family of the city, which has progressively given up its functions to larger social agencies, was bad. See Kate Kingsley Ide's "Primary Social Settlement," *Popular Science Monthly* 62 (February 1898): 542-43, 546-47. The same argument is used by Santee to oppose the Sunday School movement, which he saw

taking away another function belonging to the family. See his "Sunday School's Relation to the State," pp. 404-5. James McKeen Cattell used a similar argument to attack the role of school. For Cattell, even education is best carried out by the family in a rural setting. See his article, "The School and the Family," *Popular Science Monthly* 74 (1909): 84-96. The family reformers' conception of the city as a threat to the family can be seen as part of a broader and more generalized hatred of cities and urban life by many prominent American writers and intellectuals, according to Morton and Lucia White. See their book, *The Intellectual Versus the City: From Thomas Jefferson to Frank Lloyd Wright* (Cambridge: Harvard University Press and the M.I.T. Press, 1962). The view that rural life promoted the sense of self-worth and cooperation of family members was repeatedly voiced by Charles Loring Brace. See his *Dangerous Classes*, especially chapters 19 and 20. The view that children were a hindrance and a bother to the city family with its ostentatious and fragile furnishings to impress others was expressed by J. F. Rowe in his article, "The Family as Typical of the State," *Christian Quarterly* 7 (1875): 514-15. The praise of patriarchal authority was generally voiced in religious literature, with the authors employing quotations from scripture to support their arguments. See T[homas] DeWitt Talmadge, *The Wedding Ring* (New York and Chicago: Butler Brothers, [1886]), pp. 102-17; Rowe, "Family as Typical of the State," p. 525, and Schaff, "Influence of Christianity on the Family," pp. 473-91. For a discussion of the popular ideal of woman as a subordinate to the authority of father and husband which appeared in women's magazines of the nineteenth century, see Barbara Welter's article, "The Cult of True Womanhood: 1820-1860," *American Quarterly* 18 (1966): 151-74.

43. Taylor, "American Childhood," pp. 47-48, 52-54, and Charles W. Eliot, "Family Stocks in a Democracy," *Forum* 10 (1890): 398-99.

44. Brace believed that there was some unspecified benign element that accompanied working in the soil that promoted mental health in children, particularly girls. See his *Dangerous Classes*, pp. 400-401. Taylor saw in city life a tendency toward overspecialization, which left the personality unbalanced and subject to excesses. In addition, he equated physical health with mental health. See his article, "American Childhood," pp. 44-45, 52.

45. Rowe, "Family as Typical of the State," p. 519; Eliot, "Family Stocks," pp. 402-3; and Taylor, "American Childhood," p. 51.

46. Talmadge, *Wedding Ring*, pp. 117-32; Taylor, "American Childhood," pp. 44-55; Eliot, "Family Stocks," p. 403; and Charles Franklin Thwing and Carrie F. Butler Thwing: *The Family: An Historical and Social Study* (Boston: Lee and Sheperd, 1887), p. 164.

47. This idea became a central theme of philanthropy in the 1880s, but

was expressed as early as 1872 by Charles Loring Brace. See his *Dangerous Classes*, pp. 388-97.

48. The idea that charity was a cause of the increase in the numbers of the poor was strongly emphasized by Samuel Humphreys Gurteen, founder of the original charity organization society established in the United States (the Buffalo Charity Organization Society, established in 1877). Gurteen equated the growing ranks of America's urban poor with the unemployed plebian citizens of Imperial Rome, and equated indiscriminate material relief to Rome's free grain dole to any citizen who wanted it. He believed that the Roman grain dole had created an army of paupers, which eventually turned upon the Empire that supported them and aided in its destruction. With the specter of the 1863 New York draft riot in mind, Gurteen believed that the continued growth of material relief societies would create the same situation in the United States. See his book, *A Handbook of Charity Organization* (Buffalo: Courier Company, 1882), pp. 44-45. Gurteen's book was the major expression of early charity organization in America. An excellent brief history of early charity organization is Robert H. Bremmer's article, " 'Scientific Philanthropy,' 1873-93," *Social Service Review* 30 (1956): 168-73, and his book, *From the Depths: The Discovery of Poverty in the United States* (New York: New York University Press, 1956), pp. 46-57. Also see Roy Lubove, *The Professional Altruist: The Emergence of Social Work as a Career, 1880-1930* (Cambridge, Mass.: Harvard University Press), pp. 1-21.

49. This scheme outlines the ideal of charity organization. Reality was often different. Charity organization presupposed a willingness on the part of the older material relief societies to cooperate with the newer charity organization societies. Often, this cooperation was absent. Many of the workers in the material relief societies resented the interference of the charity organizers in their programs and were antagonistic to what they regarded as a cold and detached approach to the problems of the poor. This hostility often led charity organization societies to engage in their own material relief work directly or set up satellite material relief societies under their supervision. Material relief was a touchy subject among charity organizers. Ideally, no material relief was to be dispensed, as their motto, "not alms, but a friend," suggested (Bremmer, "Scientific Philanthropy," pp. 170-71). A concise and insightful analysis of the problems of cooperation and material relief can be found in Philip W. Ayres' article, "Relief Associations and Their Relation to Charity Organization Societies," *NCCC* 26 (1899): 359-61. The discussion section accompanying this article presented the views of a number of the leading charity organizers toward material relief. See ibid., pp. 361-68.

50. The methodology of charity organization is clearly laid out in

Gurteen's *Handbook*, pp. 120-217. Also see Bremmer, "Scientific Philanthropy," p. 171.

51. Susan I. Lesley, "Foundlings and Deserted Children," *NCCC* 8 (1881): 286; C. D. Randall, "Report of the Committee on Child-Saving Work," *NCCC* 20 (1893): 138.

52. See George I. Chace's discussion of Charles Loring Brace's paper, "The 'Placing Out' Plan for Homeless and Vagrant Children," *NCCC* 3 (1876): 147. Also see Lyman P. Alden's discussion of Sarah B. Cooper's article, "The Kindergarten as a Child-Saving Work," *NCCC* 9 (1883): 140.

53. Louise Wolcott, "Treatment of Poor Widows with Dependent Children," *NCCC* 15 (1888): 137-40.

54. M. M'G. Dana, in his article, "The Care and Disposal of Dependent Children," *NCCC* 15 (1888): 241, strongly advocated environmental change as a technique of child-saving work. Alfred T. White's article, "Better Homes for Workingmen," *NCCC* 12 (1885): 365-82, is notable not only as a pioneer in the literature of housing reform but is also an early attempt to define the minimum income necessary to obtain decent housing. White recommended minimum housing legislation as a form of preventive therapy to avoid the evils of delinquent and criminal children raised in bad housing. Also see R. W. Hill's article, "The Children of Shinbone Alley,'" *NCCC* 14 (1887): 229-35, which is the most comprehensive argument for environmental reform in child-saving work written in the 1880s found in this survey.

55. Constance Mackenzie, in her article, "Free Kindergartens," *NCCC* 13 (1886): 48-52, noted that the kindergarten movement in the United States began in the mid-1870s. White's article, "Better Homes for Workingmen," inaugurated the housing reform movement when it appeared in 1885, about a decade after the kindergarten movement. For the virtues kindergarten was believed to hold, see R. Heber Newton, "The Bearing of the Kindergarten on the Prevention of Crime," *NCCC* 13 (1886): 53-58, and Sarah B. Cooper, "The Kindergarten as a Child-Saving Work," *NCCC* 9 (1882): 130-38.

56. "The Influence of Manual Training on Character," *NCCC* 15 (1888): 247-58.

57. "School and the Family," pp. 84-96. For a comprehensive presentation of the use of educational institutions to overcome deficient home environments, see William T. Harris' article, "Compulsory Education in Relation to Crime and Social Morals," *NCCC* 12 (1885): 228-40.

58. "Presidential Address," *NCCC* 10 (1884): 15.

59. Ibid., p. 18.

60. Ibid.

61. Mona Carid, while not a member of this scholarly group, did use the findings of the proponents of the matriarchal-origin view to support her contention that the present state of women in society was not necessarily normal, that patriarchal domination was late in development in the evolution of the family, and that the variety of family patterns in the past suggested a wider possibility of modification of the contemporary family than opponents of women's rights would admit. See her two-part article, "The Emancipation of the Family," *North American Review* 150 (1890): 692-705, and ibid., 151 (1890): 22-37.

62. Samuel Dike would periodically call for a redirection of scholarly attention toward more practical family problems than speculation about the origins and development of the family as an institution. See for instance, his "Problems of the Family," *Century* 39 (1890): 385-86, 395, and his article, "The Problems of the Family in the United States," *Contemporary Review* 64 (1893): 728, 734-35. Also see Ide, "Primary Social Settlement," pp. 535-36.

63. "Facts as to Divorce in New England." This was one of a series of lectures in Joseph Cook's Boston Monday Lecture Series. The speech was printed in the *Boston Evening Transcript*, 25 January 1881, p. 8.

64. Biographical details of Dike's early life can be found in an unpublished autobiography in the *Samuel Warren Dike Papers* at the Library of Congress. Also see Dike's report, "A Review of Fifteen Years: Report of the Corresponding Secretary," *Report of the National Divorce Reform League for the Year Ending December 31, 1895* (Boston: Everett Press Company, 1896), pp. 506. A good biography of Dike was written by William L. O'Neill, "Samuel W. Dike and the Hazards of Moral Reform," *Vermont History* 35 (1967): 160-68.

65. "Some Aspects of the Divorce Question," *Princeton Review* 60 (1884): 169-90.

66. "Important Features of the Divorce Question: Facts and Remarks About them," *Homiletic Review* 10 (1885): 391.

67. Carroll D. Wright, ed. (Washington, D. C.: U. S. Bureau of Labor, 1889).

68. This is O'Neill's opinion as expressed in his article, "Dike and the Hazards of Reform," p. 163. O'Neill's gauge of Dike's influence was his correspondence. I have examined this correspondence and concur with his opinion. Dike's correspondence in the 1890s is virtually a list of notable reformers and social scientists at the end of the nineteenth century, among them James Bryce, Franklin H. Giddings, Albion Small, and G. Stanley Hall. His relations with Theodore D. Woolsey, President of Yale, and Carrol D. Wright, Commissioner of the Bureau of Statistics and a pioneer figure in the gathering of social statistics are especially close. Dike was a

member of many of the social science organizations of the time, often as a charter member. Most of his correspondence is concentrated between 1885 and about 1905, which roughly corresponds to the period of Dike's greatest influence.

69. *The Family.*

70. Ibid., pp. 137-43.

71. This is not to be taken to mean that marriage between husband and wife was not seen as a form of regulating individual desire. It was, but the Thwings implied that the divine purposes of marriage included perpetuation of the race and the nurture and training of children (*The Family,*. pp. 92-94). Additionally, they attacked what they saw as a growing number of "boarding-house" marriages, with husbands married to their businesses and functionless and idle wives who viewed the responsibilities of parenthood with distaste. They viewed such marriages as conducive of selfishness and irresponsibility (ibid., p. 164).

72. The basis of this contention was a reinterpretation of the doctrines of St. Paul, which stressed the priority of the creation of man (1 Tim., ii., 13), the fact that the woman and not man was deceived in the first transgression (1 Tim., ii., 14), and the belief that woman was made for man, not the reverse (1 Cor., xi., 9). The Thwings reject the literal interpretation of these passages as they are written, which they admit would lead to concluding that women are inferior to men. While the Thwings believed these views expressed a level of opinion in advance of his age, they believed Paul's views to be colored by the prejudices of his times and inappropriate in modern society. See their book, *The Family*, pp. 112-18.

73. Ibid., pp. 120-65, 169-70.

74. Ibid., pp. 162-66.

75. Ibid., pp. 152-202.

76. Ibid., p. 110.

77. I am not suggesting that there were no alternative models of family life proposed, but rather, in terms of the literature surveyed, that models of family life outside the standard model of the monogamous, marriage-sanctioned family were effectively beneath discussion in a dispassionate way within the pages of "respectable" journals. There was, for instance, no round-table discussion of Mormon polygamy, with advocates allowed to present their views as well as opponents, although one article by Susa Young Gates, one of Brigham Young's daughters, did paint a nostalgic and favorable portrait of childhood in polygamy on the eve of its extinction. See Gates' article, "Family Life Among the Mormons," *North American Review* 150 (1890): 339-50. Even here the article went to great lengths to point out the similarities of Mormon family life to the generally accepted pattern of family life.

II

SOCIOLOGY AND THE FAMILY IN THE PROGRESSIVE ERA, 1890-1920

Ronald L. Howard _____

The three decades from 1890 to 1920 witnessed the rise and decline of a widespread social movement to solve the problems created by industrialization in America. These problems were neither new nor suddenly discovered. They had accompanied the process of industrialization and had grown with it. In the course of these decades, however, popular attitudes toward these problems and the means proposed to solve them changed. No longer were they regarded as simple matters of moral reform. Instead, they came to be viewed as the product of industrialization and urbanization, for which programs of social reform and social legislation alone offered relief. The family had emerged as a topic of such moral concern in the 1870s and 1880s. After 1890, the family became the object of social concern, as a victim of the forces of industrialization and urbanization. By the eve of World War I, this social concern for the family broadened to include its social environment of neighborhood and community. Finally, the problems of the family came to be seen as components of major dislocations of the entire social order resulting from industrialization and urbanization.

It was in this environment of broadening social concern that sociology established itself as an academic discipline. In 1890, sociology was vaguely defined and nowhere more than a course offering at a few colleges and universities in the United States.[1] By 1920, sociology was firmly established as an academic discipline at most colleges and universities in the United States; and two universities, Chicago and Columbia, had together produced over one hundred Ph.D.'s in sociology.[2]

The establishment of sociology as an academic discipline during these years can be viewed as the process of differentiation from other academic and professional disciplines. The most important was the separation of sociology from the field of social work. Through most of the decade of the 1890s, it was difficult to distinguish between sociology and social work. Sociology in the 1890s was more a potential than an actual discipline. Lacking a distinct methodology and clearly defined fields of inquiry, sociologists devoted their efforts to defining the nature of their discipline and its boundaries. Little sociological research was produced before the twentieth century.[3]

Within this state of formlessness, sociology appeared to be an attractive answer to the conceptual problems of charity workers. They were increasingly impressed with the interdependence of social pathologies and their suspected relationship with the workings of society at large. Charity workers hoped that sociology would reveal the inner nature of the workings of society, which they believed would immediately make clear the methods by which social problems could be solved. In a very real sense, the study of society was seen to be an integral part of social reform.[4]

This idea was enhanced by the fact that many of the early sociologists were themselves social reformers or came from backgrounds particularly congenial to reform. The faculty of the first sociology department at the University of Chicago serves as an excellent example. Albion Small (1854-1926), department chairman, was a graduate of Newton Theological Seminary. Although his subsequent contributions to sociology were to enhance and contribute to the separation of sociology from social work, he remained congenial to programs of general social reform. His associate, Charles Richmond Henderson (1848-1908), was also a seminary graduate, a practicing Baptist minister who eventually became chaplain of the University of Chicago and held a sociology chair in that university's divinity school. His academic career was devoted to social reform and philanthropic work. A third department member, George Edgar Vincent (1864-1941), was a son of the founder of the Chautauqua movement. Like his father, George Vincent devoted his career to the promotion of educational reform. Of the original Chicago faculty, only William Isaac Thomas (1863-1947) came to the department without a background of either theological training or social reform experience. Social activism by academic sociologists was not confined to the sociology faculty at Chicago. Edward Alsworth Ross (1866-1951), first at Stanford and later at Wisconsin, remained a perennial advocate of numerous programs of social reform, as did Charles A. Ellwood (1873-1946) at Missouri.[5]

After the turn of the century, both sociology and social work experienced professionalization, which by 1920 separated them into two distinct disciplines. At the heart of this growing divergence was a fundamental difference in the professional images that sociologists and social workers developed of themselves and their activities. Both groups saw the professionalization of their respective fields as making them more scientific, but they shared no uniform conception of what "scientific" meant. For the social worker, becoming scientific was seen in terms of modelling their profession upon the profession of medicine, especially on its clinical methodology of diagnosis, the prescription of treatment on the basis of diagnosis, and careful observation and recording of the results of treatment.[6] The sociologist viewed the development of a scientific sociology in terms of pure empirical research into social phenomena, free from the biases of moral scruples or cultural ethnocentrism.[7] These differing conceptions of the meaning of becoming scientific led to divergent professional goals for the two disciplines. Sociologists came to view the goal of their profession as social knowledge, while social workers saw their goal as social therapy.

It must be emphasized, however, that this distinction between sociology and social work was neither clear-cut nor absolute, particularly in the case of sociology. Rather, it should be understood in terms of the formation of two distinct professional ideologies to justify professional autonomy. Like other ideologies, those of sociologists and social workers tended to exaggerate, rather than accurately to depict the differences between them.[8]

In terms of the family, the relationship between sociologists and social workers followed a different pattern than that of sociology and social work in general. In this area of common interest, the relationship between sociologists and social workers remained one of interdependence, rather than of growing autonomy. It was a relationship dominated by the social workers rather than the sociologists. This domination reflected the central position the family enjoyed within the field of social work. The family remained the central focus of concern for social work throughout this period, and the preservation of the family became the major justification for the existence of family case work. The situation was different in the case of sociology, where the family was not a major field of study. This fact can be illustrated by examining the issues of the *American Journal of Sociology* during its initial twenty-five years, from 1895 to 1920. Of the approximately eleven hundred articles printed in this journal during this period, less than forty specifically dealt with the family, and of these, thirty appeared in one volume as reprints of the third annual conference of the American Sociological Society, which was devoted to the family.[9] Of the doctoral dissertations completed in sociology before 1920, only eleven were devoted to the family or related topics.[10]

The disparity in the level of interest in the family between social workers and sociologists is evidence of a fundamental difference in perspective not readily apparent in the literature of these two fields. Both social workers and sociologists wrote textbooks about the family that are remarkable more for their similarity than for their differences. Virtually all of them followed the model of a family text inaugurated by the Thwings' work in 1887 and employed a similar two-part structure. One section of the text was devoted to a history of the origins and development of the family, and the other section was devoted to a discussion of the contemporary family and the problems it faced.[11] Based on their respective presentations of the history and development of the family, social workers and sociologists developed analyses that exhibit no real differences. In this respect, the family textbooks of both social workers and sociologists served to preserve the legacy of the early evolutionist scholars of the family. Little was added to the historical analyses of the early family scholars. Their analyses of the contemporary family and its problems, in many respects similar, reveal fundamental distinctions that reflect developments in the larger general fields of sociology and social work between 1890 and 1920. By the end of this period, the family would become the focus of techniques of diagnosis and treatment of social case work. Family preservation would become a professional goal, part of the disciplinary value system and, as such, above critical analysis. The goal of family preservation intimated a view of the family as a fragile and endangered species, one that required much study and observation to protect it from extinction.[12] Within sociology, an opposite conception of the family developed, one which stressed the resilience and adaptability of the family to social change.

To be sure, sociologists were not indifferent to social problems faced by the family, but their concern was usually shown in ways that their emerging professional image as detached, scientific students of society could readily accommodate. From their perspective, the family, by its very adaptability to social change, did not provide a good foundation for launching programs of social reform. The family's conditions could be improved and the problems it faced lightened through programs of social reform, but the family itself was not an agency of social change. The family was not a creator of its social environment but a captive of it.[13]

This conception of the family as a strong rather than a weak institution first made its appearance in the course of the debate over divorce, which led to the alienation of the sociologists from the moral reformers.[14] The divorce debate had been a topic of increasing public concern through most of the second half of the nineteenth century, and sociologists early favored a liberal attitude. After the publication of the government report in 1889 on the statistics of marriage and divorce, the debate was raised to a new level of sophistication. No longer was it merely a matter of moral rhetoric; it had become the object of factual statistical analysis.

The first of the major sociological studies based on the census bureau's 1889 report of marriage and divorce statistics was Walter F. Willcox's (1861-1964) doctoral dissertation, *The Divorce Problem: A Study in Statistics*, published in 1891. The concluding pages of this work developed a conception of the family as a strong institution. Having disposed of the popular belief that the rising divorce rate reflected increased immorality and lax divorce laws, Willcox provided nine working hypotheses to account for the rise. The majority of these were not couched in moral terms, but reflected larger social developments that he saw as progressive and socially beneficial, such as the growing emancipation of women, the growing popularity of the law, and the increasing implementation of legal remedies for personal problems. The solution to the problem of divorce would not be found through the enactment of legislation, but through the spread of moral education, focused upon the responsibilities of family life, not the evils of divorce.[15] The last page of his study makes clear that Willcox saw the family undergoing a process of reconstruction, in which women would come to have new rights and duties, and other family relations would have to be adjusted to meet the new status of women. The final remedy then was not legislation, but education and study to determine what new rights and duties of the new family form were more appropriate to democratic society.[16]

Willcox's position came to represent the views of a number of sociologists, particularly after the turn of the century. His idea that divorce was a sign of the family as an institution in transition was elaborated by George Elliott Howard (1849-1928) in the concluding sections of his massive work, *A History of Matrimonial Institutions*, published in 1904.[17] In keeping with the new self-image of the sociologist as the scientific student of sociology, Howard regarded all appeals to scripture for guidance in family affairs as useless. Instead, marriage and the family had to be studied in connection with actual conditions of married life.[18]

Howard believed that the contemporary family was in a state of transition. Divorce was indicative of this transition,[19] reflecting the growth of women's independence.[20] While he conceded that the movement for women's rights could, upon occasion, involve excessive assertion of individual rights over responsibilities, he regarded this as an inevitable price of social progress.[21] He believed that the transformation of society led to an assertion of individual freedom, but he rejected the moral conservative's notion that such freedom was accompanied by a growth in social irresponsibility. Rather, increasing individual freedom had been accompanied by a growth in collective responsibility, illustrated by the growth of social legislation in housing, factory, and labor conditions.[22]

Howard viewed the problems of congested urban life, slums, and tenement life as destructive of the family. It was in this light that he perceived the failure of employers to supply family heads with a living wage as a far greater threat to the family than divorce, as it necessitated the employment of wives and children, effectively breaking up the family.[23] Yet he remained optimistic about the future of the family. He saw the continuing development of urban transportation systems as a remedy that would help by decentralizing congested cities and believed that economic threats to the family could be eradicated through legislation.[24]

The problems of the family, then, were a part of the difficulties facing the larger society. The family of the future would emphasize the growth of children's and individual family members' rights as the family bonds of coercion were transformed into bonds of affection and persuasion. Citing a study of John R. Commons (1866-1944), Howard noted that the authority of the parent over the child had already been effectively limited by charity workers in child-saving work.[25] Family stability was ultimately a function of enlightened public sentiment, not legislation. Like Willcox, he believed that the foundation of such stability could be provided by education for the responsibilities of married life.[26]

The most detailed study of divorce by a sociologist during this period was James P. Lichtenberger's (1870-1953) *Divorce: A Study in Social Causation*.[27] Lichtenberger's book came to represent the final form of prevailing sociological opinion on divorce and, indirectly, on the family. Building upon the analyses of Willcox and Howard, Lichtenberger regarded divorce as an effect, not a cause, of instability. Like them, he saw economic pressures and the growing independence of women as causes of the increase in the divorce rate. He went further, however, to suggest that to the extent that the increase in divorce reflected the refusal of women to accept prevailing double standards of marital morality, divorce could be regarded as a sign of family health.[28] Divorce was a symptom of social readjustment that would abate once a new social consensus on marital rights and privileges was achieved. Significantly, Lichtenberger declined to predict that such a consensus would be achieved, only that the achievement of such a consensus would be reflected in the decline in the divorce rate. That the family might remain within a permanent state of transition, with an attendant high divorce rate, was no cause for alarm to Lichtenberger. The family was the natural, inevitable result of human sentiments of mutual attraction and preference. Its historical survival reflected the durability and persistence of these sentiments.[29]

Most of the moral reformers who viewed divorce as a threat to the continued survival of the family took an opposite view of both the family and society in general. Developing their viewpoint from fixed principles, their opinions were not really amenable to the influence of the empirical findings of sociologists like Willcox, Howard, and Lichtenberger.[30] For them, marriage was a sacrament, and should be beyond the interference of secular authority. The family was the cornerstone of society, whose existence was threatened by the dissolution of the sacred bonds that tied it together. Seeing the family, then, in the light of religious sanctions, they believed internal family relationships were divinely ordained. Although their conceptions of these relationships varied according to scriptural interpretation, the moral reformers uniformly believed that they were permanent. This belief generated a conception of the family as a fixed rather than a flexible institution, one that either thrived under the proper conditions or disintegrated under adverse conditions. Since the family was usually viewed by moral reformers as the keystone of society, the fate of society was tied to it.[31] Thus, the emotional investment of the moral reformers in the family was high, which serves to explain the vehemence and alarm with which they described the divorce threat. Its continued rise threatened not only the family but the continued existence of society as well. Unless the trends were reversed or stopped altogether, the future of civilization was in grave doubt.

It is not surprising then that the reaction of the moral reformers to the sociologists was hostile. That this reaction did not emerge in the wake of Willcox's book in 1891 but developed after the turn of the century is due to two factors. First, Willcox's study was primarily a statistical analysis addressed to an audience familiar with statistical techniques, an audience largely nonexistent in the 1890s.[32] Second, as has been noted, family sociology enjoyed the patronage of Samuel W. Dike. Between Dike's advocacy of sociology as the science that could find remedies for the family's ills and the moral conservatives' ignorance of Willcox's study, sociology remained outside the divorce debate through the 1890s.

This situation changed after the turn of the century with the publication of G. E. Howard's study. Unlike Willcox, Howard was a scholar with an established reputation. His resignation from Stanford University in 1901 in protest of the dismissal of his controversial colleague, Edward Alsworth Ross, raised him to national prominence, and the publication of his work was hailed as a major scholarly event. In addition, he wrote a number of articles affirming his advocacy of free divorce that attracted the attention of the moral reformers.[33] From the middle of the first decade of the twentieth century, the relations between sociologists and moral reformers became increasingly antagonistic. One of the first victims of this hostility was Samuel Dike himself, for much of his professional energy had been expended in trying to make the National Divorce Reform League a bridge between the sociologists and the moral reformers.[34]

The ambiguity of Dike's position is reflected in his writings on divorce and the family, which bear earmarks of the viewpoints of both the sociologists and the moral reformers. The family and its preservation constantly remained at the center of Dike's attention.[35] He saw the family beset with numerous moral and environmental afflictions, yet his writing lacks the note of impending doom characteristic of moral reformers.[36] On the other hand, his work did not reflect the optimistic conviction of the sociologists that the family was a sturdy and flexible institution that would adapt to new social conditions. He was unable to look upon divorce simply as a symptom of social adjustment, but he was equally unable to advocate the promotion of programs of legislative divorce restriction.[37] His belief in the family as the cornerstone of the state remained above critical scrutiny, but his ultimate remedy for family salvation was not religious dogma, but scientific, sociological study.[38] Ironically, his understanding and comprehension of sociology was limited and, after the turn of the century, dated. In particular, Dike was not in sympathy with the increasing interest in the field of social psychology, which he saw coming to dominate the field of sociology.[39] In its place, he advocated the return to a sociology primarily based upon structural rather than functional analysis. The tone of his criticism suggests that incomprehension, rather than theoretical opposition, lay at the heart of his dislike of social psychology.[40]

Dike did correctly comprehend the growing importance of social psychology to sociology. By the end of the first decade of the twentieth century, social psychology had emerged as the dominant field of sociology and played a crucial role in the formation of sociology's professional self-image. The basic contention of social psychology that society was a distinctly human phenomenon, the product of human interaction, proved to be instrumental in helping sociology divest itself of evolutionary conceptions borrowed from the biological sciences. With the development of the social-psychological conception of society, sociology was able to provide itself with a distinct theoretical perspective that gave credibility to its claim to professional autonomy.[41]

The influence of social psychology extended to sociologists' conceptions of the family after the turn of the century and centered upon the traditionally recognized function of the family as an agency for the socialization of the young and the development of parental character. Social psychology engendered a perspective of the family that increasingly emphasized its function as an agency of socialization. With the publication of Charles Horton Cooley's (1864-1929) *Social Organization*, sociological attention shifted from the family as the agency of socialization to the function of socialization itself. The effect of this development was to divest the family of its traditional position as both a unique and a strategic social institution. The family would remain an important social institution to sociologists, but it would not be a uniquely important institution, whose major functions were nontransferable. This new social-psychological perspective enhanced sociologists' general conception of the family as a flexible and adaptable institution.

Aspects of this new perspective can be discerned as early as 1901 in Arthur Fairbanks' (1864-1944) textbook, *Introduction to Sociology*. Building upon the traditional conception of the family as the agency of childhood socialization and the development of parental character, Fairbanks went on to suggest that the measure of social progress was not the development of social institutions but the moral heritage children received from their parents. Civilization and progress were essentially social attitudes and sentiments, not social institutions.[42]

Four years later, Frank W. Blackmar (1864-1931), in his textbook, *Elements of Sociology*, more explicitly developed this concept by emphasizing that the sentiment of love, a product of family culture, was the essential ingredient of society; it was the basis of the art of living together. In Blackmar's conception, society was not the evolutionary enlargement of family structure and authority relations, but the expansion of the basic sentiment of family cohesion.[43]

Charles Horton Cooley provided the fully developed enlargement of the social-psychological perspective of the family in his work, *Social Organization*.[44] For Cooley, sentiments were not only the essential quality of society, but were the essential quality of humanity itself.[45] What had been the function of socialization was enlarged by Cooley to be nothing less than the function of becoming human. In addition, Cooley separated this function from the family. He ascribed the function of becoming human to primary groups, which included the family. Street gangs and peasant village communities could also be primary groups, either in addition to or in lieu of the family.[46] This essential observation serves to explain why Cooley was struck with the vitality rather than the pathology of slum-tenement family life, for what he was seeing was similar to the observations of an increasing number of settlement-house workers. Even under the most adverse of environmental conditions, human development went on. Slum families did not exist as totally autonomous entities; they interacted with each other in the larger primary group of the neighborhood or the street gang. Such interaction implied that these other primary groups could supplement the family in the fundamentally human process of socialization.[47]

The emphasis Cooley placed upon the varieties of socialization and the role of the family, while optimistic, is not to be interpreted as indifference toward family problems or disinterest in family reform. In many ways, Cooley's conceptions heightened concern of sociologists for the problems of the family. Primary groups, such as street gangs, were pathological; and the socialization that took place within such primary groups produced individuals who shared their antisocial attitudes.[48] In addition, Cooley noted the difficulties individuals socialized within primary groups suffered in trying to accommodate themselves to the more complex and depersonalized relationships of secondary group organizations. Yet, the solution of these problems could not exclusively focus upon the family. It was a problem of social organization in general.[49] For Cooley, the problems of the family were tied into the problems of socialization and adaptation to ever more complex social forms.

This point was reinforced in 1914 in John M. Gillette's (1866-1949) textbook, *The Family and Society*. Gillette discounted the fear of many traditional family reformers over the loss of family independence, for the family was not an independent social unit. Rather, the family was bound up in a network of social interdependence with other social groups, such that its problems and those of society as a whole were intertwined.[50]

While the viewpoints of Cooley and Gillette came to characterize the maturing sociological conception of the family, it was not shared by all sociologists. The most notable exception was Charles A. Ellwood (1873-1946). Ellwood was one of the major pioneers in the developing field of social psychology and an enthusiastic advocate of Charles Horton Cooley and his work.[51] At the same time, he was a devout Christian who shared many of the fears and anxieties of conventional moral reformers concerning the future of the family and, like them, became an opponent of divorce.[52] These conflicting perspectives were translated into his analysis of the family. Although Ellwood extensively used Cooley's concepts of the primary group, he made the family more important than other primary groups by endowing it with unique social functions that could not be transferred to other social institutions.

Building upon Blackmar's idea that the sentiment of family love was the foundation of the art of living together, Ellwood translated this sentiment into the term "family altruism" and contended that social progress was congruent with the attempts of mankind to extend family altruism to larger forms of social organization. The family became the unique repository of this sentiment. With the moral reformers, Ellwood believed that social developments that threatened the family threatened society itself.[53] In light of this perspective, he viewed the family as a precious social resource. Reproduction and the rearing of children were social responsibilities that had primacy over individual rights, even those of the parents themselves. Divorce was the socially unjustified elevation of personal considerations over social responsibilities. Childless families, whatever merit the couples that composed them might otherwise have, necessarily had to be regarded as social failures.[54] Ellwood was realistic enough to believe, as did most of his colleagues, that the attempt to legislate morality was largely an exercise in futility.[55] Still, his religious and ethical sentiments prevented him from accepting the rising rate of divorce passively, and he became a steadfast, if not enthusiastic, advocate of legislative restrictions on divorce.[56] His over-all assessment of family problems was more in keeping with the general body of sociological opinion. Though it was right to try to stem the rising tide of divorce through legislation, the enduring remedy for Ellwood, as for Lichtenberger, Blackmar, Howard, and Fairbanks, was social education for the responsibilities of married life.[57]

Though Ellwood was unable to conceive of divorce simply as a symptom of social adjustment, he did see it as an evil symptomatic of a larger general breakdown of family life in industrial society. Ellwood, along with many sociologists and social reformers of the Progressive Era, believed that the problems of family instability were tied to the greater problems of the society as a whole, for which a thoroughgoing reconstruction of the moral, industrial, and political spheres of American life would provide the only lasting remedy.[58] His social-psychological perspective viewed such a reconstruction in terms of social sentiments. His religious background translated this perspective into a moral imperative. As a result, Ellwood devoted much of his subsequent career to writing a new religion for humanity, much as Comte had attempted to do a century before, which tried to combine the qualities of religious conviction and motivation with the insights of modern sociology.[59]

The social-psychological conceptions of the family developed by Blackmar, Gillette, Ellwood, and Cooley spotlighted the role of the family as the major institution of socialization. This view was further developed by William I. Thomas and Florian W. Znaniecki (1882-1958) in their work, *The Polish Peasant in Europe and America*, the most important family study of this period.[60] The result of nearly a decade of research, *The Polish Peasant* was far more than a simple family study monograph.[61] In a broad sense, the work was a study of the disintegrative effects on Polish peasants culture of rapid social change caused by industrialization and urbanization. This topic was of crucial interest to sociologists and social workers at the time, for it directly related to problems of immigration and assimilation, to the adaptation of individuals and groups to social change, and to the nature of social change itself. The strategic nature of the central topic of *The Polish Peasant* helps to explain its profound influence upon American sociology. The view of Polish family and community life that this work described was a dark and foreboding one. Polish peasant culture consisted of primary group organizations.[62] Family and community were closely tied together in a mutually dependent relationship that was deteriorating as social organization in both Poland and America evolved into the larger and more impersonal secondary group patterns of industrialized societies. The essential nature of this deterioration was "social disorganization," which they defined as "a decrease of the influence of existing rules of behavior upon individual members of the group."[63] Although they noted that the migration of peasant families from rural to urban settings was a general cause of social disorganization, the essential process was one in which these environmental changes induced shifts in the values of the individuals experiencing them. The source of social disorganization was the conflict between the values associated with the old and new social environments.[64]

The Polish peasant was equipped with values that translated personal desires into family desires.[65] This transformation of individual desires to family desires was not maintained by the family alone; the peasant village community played a crucial role in supporting and augmenting family values.[66] At the same time, the peasant village community was inward-facing and isolated the family from the larger social world outside the village community.[67] Peasant families and communities were interdependent institutions; and in the absence of the village community, the peasant family was hard pressed to maintain its solidarity. Isolated from the village community, either in Poland or in the United States, the ability of families to subordinate individualized desires to family aspirations broke down. In the absence of family opposition to individual family members' new sense of individual desire and ambition stimulated by the new urban social environment, family breakdown was marked simply by a decline of family interest. If the family tried to oppose individual family members' new sense of individualism, open hostility and antisocial behavior resulted.[68] In an interesting way, Thomas and Znaniecki confirmed some of the moral conservatives' fears of excessive individualism. In the new social environment of urban America, the values of individualism and competition overrode the old values that had emphasized the promotion of the family's welfare, and the family did indeed break down. Contrary to the hopes of the moral conservatives, however, schemes to reinstill values of family primacy were unworkable. Family reorganization could take place, but only on a new basis that recognized individual desires and consciously harmonized them with other family members' desires for the pursuit of common family goals.[69] Primary group formation and maintenance was a spontaneous, reflexive process.[70] Once this form of social organization had broken down, its replacement had to be a form of rational and conscious organization. There could be no return to the past.

Though their study was confined to Polish peasant communites in Poland and urban America, Thomas and Znaniecki suggested that the process of primary group breakdown and eventual reorganization along consciously rational lines was a universal one. Similar processes were at work within the rural communities of America as individuals and families moved to the cities in search of work.[71] For this reason, the problems of disorganization and reorganization the Polish community was undergoing were symptomatic of a major social transformation that would eventually involve the entirety of mankind.[72] It was toward the study and resolution of such problems that social science necessarily had to direct itself.[73]

The Polish Peasant represents both the end of one era in family sociology and the beginning of another. In one sense, the work reflected the rising interest of the Progressive Era in the concerns for the loss of community life as a major casualty of the process of industrialization. By the end of the first decade of the twentieth century, settlement house workers had come to view their primary task as one of preserving or restoring urban neighborhood communities. Increasingly, they had come to recognize that family problems were inseparable from the problems of the neighborhood community; the survival of one was dependent upon the health of the other. These views were echoed by most sociologists of this period, who saw the solution of family instability in terms of the development of a new social consensus that recognized both the individuality of family members and their responsibilities to the larger society. In another sense, Thomas and Znaniecki's emphasis upon the need to study the internal and subjective processes of social disorganization anticipated the growing preoccupation of family sociologists in the 1920s and 1930s with the internal relationships of family interaction, rather than the external relationships of the family with larger institutions of society.

NOTES

1. See Floyd House's book, *The Development of Sociology* (New York: McGraw-Hill Book Company, Inc., 1936), pp. 224-25, and Jesse Bernard's article, "The History and Prospects of Sociology in the United States," in George A. Lundberg, Read Bain, and Nels Anderson, eds., *Trends in American Sociology* (New York: Harper and Brothers, 1929), pp. 15-18. Also see Daniel Fulcomer's article, "Instruction in Sociology in Institutions of Learning," *NCCC* 21 (1894): 67-79.

2. Bernard, "History and Prospects," pp. 48-71.

3. The ambiguous and vague character of sociology during the 1890s can be seen in the course and department descriptions in Frank L. Tolman's "Study of Sociology in Institutions of Learning in the United States," *American Journal of Sociology* 7 (1901): 797-838, 8 (1902): 85-121, 251-72, 531-58 (hereinafter referred to as *AJS*. Also see Albion Small's article, "Fifty Years of Sociology in the United States," *AJS* 21 (1916): 802, and Bernard, "History and Prospects," pp. 11-15.

4. In the *AJS* from 1895 to 1900 (volumes 1-5), 97 articles were devoted to social theory, and another 97 articles were devoted to political, economic, and social reform of the total of 220 articles. Put in another way, approximately 88 percent of the articles during these years reflected this interest in social theory and reform. Only 27 articles, or approximately 12 percent, made use of either empirical or statistical methods. See footnote 9 for a discussion of the methodology used to categorize these articles. For a presentation of the social worker's perspective of sociology, see Frank J. Bruno's *Trends in Social Work as Reflected in the Proceedings of the National Conference of Social Work, 1874-1946* (New York: Columbia University Press, 1948), pp. 133-38. Also see the sections on sociology in

NCCC 21 (1894): 67-93, 313-20, and *NCCC* 22 (1895): 110-49, particularly
Walter F. Willcox's article, "The Relation of Statistics to Social Science,"
NCCC 21 (1894): 86-93.

5. See Robert E. L. Faris' *Chicago Sociology, 1920-1932* (San Francisco:
Chandler Publishing Company, 1967), pp. 11-19. An excellent biography
of Edward Alsworth Ross is Julius Weinberg's *Edward Alsworth Ross and
the Sociology of Progressivism* (Madison: State Historical Society of
Wisconsin, 1972), particularly pp. 123-48. A good short account of Charles
A. Ellwood's life can be found in Harry Elmer Barnes' article, "Charles
Abram Ellwood: Founder of Scientific Psychological Sociology," Harry
Elmer Barnes, ed., *An Introduction to the History of Sociology* (Chicago:
University of Chicago Press, 1948), pp. 853-68. Also see Howard Odum,
American Sociology: The Story of Sociology in the United States through
[sic] *1950* (New York: Longmans, Green, and Company, 1951), pp. 128-31,
and Heinz Maus, *A Short History of Sociology* (London: Routledge and
Kegan Paul, 1962), pp. 104-5.

6. A good discussion of this development in social work can be found
in Roy Lubove, *The Professional Altruist: The Emergence of Social Work
as a Career, 1880-1930* (Cambridge, Mass.: Harvard University Press,
1965), pp. 22-54. A particularly insightful use of the analogy of medicine
to scientific social work is developed in Charles Frederick Weller's article,
"Relief Work and Prevention: Relief Work and Preventive Philanthropies
as Related to Charity Organization," *NCCC* 29 (1902): 265-77.

7. For an excellent discussion of the emergence of empirical traditions
in sociology during this period, see Hamilton Cravens' article, "The
Abandonment of Evolutionary Social Theory in America: The Impact of
Academic Professionalization upon American Sociological Theory, 1890-
1920," *American Studies* 12 ([Fall] 1971): 5-31.

8. The concept of professional ideology and its role in helping to define
professional autonomy is discussed in Wilbert E. Moore's and Gerald W.
Rosenblum's book, *The Professions: Roles and Rules* (New York: Russell
Sage Foundation, 1970), pp. 36-38, 51-83. Also see Everett C. Hughes'
"Professions," in Kenneth S. Lynn and the editors of Daedalus, eds.,
The Professions in America (Boston: Houghton Mifflin Company, 1965),
pp. 1-14, and Irving Louis Horowitz' article, "Mainliners and Marginals:
The Human Shape of Sociological Theory," in his *Professing Sociology:
Studies in the Life Cycle of Social Science* (Chicago: Aldine Publishing
Company, 1968), pp. 195-220. Note particularly pp. 198-201.

9. Articles were defined by the annual index that accompanied each of
the annual volumes of the *AJS*. If the index listed an item as an article, it
was so classified. As a result, books, which were upon occasion reprinted or

printed as article series, were not listed as a single entry but were listed as a group of articles. Using this criterion as a basis for defining what an article was, the total number of articles for the first twenty five years of the *AJS* was 1,094 articles. The total number of articles that by examination of their content were determined to have dealt with the family or a related topic, such as marriage, was thirty-nine. That such a criterion of classification is subjective is readily admitted, but unavoidable. The cumulative indexes of the *AJS* were of no help as the criteria of categorical inclusion varied from cumulative index to index, and an article included in one cumulative index could well be excluded from the next, or the reverse might occur.

10. This figure was obtained by checking the listings under the keywords, "child," "children," "divorce," "desertion," "familial," "family," "father," "marital," "marriage," "mother," "parents," and "parental" in the section on sociology in the *Comprehensive Dissertation Index*, Vol. 17: *The Social Sciences*; 37 vols. (Ann Arbor: Xerox University Microfilms, 1973), 17: 396-99, 463, 478, 507-13, 515, 616-19, 644-45, 684-85. Four of these dissertations, Ahmed Shukri's "Mohammedan Law of Marriage and Divorce" (Columbia University, 1916), Ernest Frank Mc-Gregor's "Marriage and the Family among the Early Hebrews" (Yale University, 1916), David Russell Lee's "Child Life, Adolescence, and Marriage in Greek New Comedy in the Comedies of Plautus: A Study of the Relations Represented as Existing between Parents and Their Children" (University of Wisconsin, 1907), and Chilton Latham Powell's "English Domestic Relations, 1487-1653: A Study of Matrimony and Family Life in Theory and Practice as Revealed by the Literature, Law, and History of the Period" (Columbia University, 1916), were historical in nature and reflect the older scholarly traditions of family study of the nineteenth century. A second group of four dissertations reflect the moral concerns and problems of the family: Walter F. Willcox's "Divorce Problem: A Study in Statistics" (Columbia University, 1891), James P. Lichtenberger's "Divorce: A Study in Social Causation" (Columbia University, 1909), Earle Eubank's "Study of Family Desertion" (University of Chicago, 1915), and John Alston Ellis' "Lax Marital Relations in the United States" (Southern Baptist Theological Seminary, 1917). Robert Colt Chapin's "Standard of Living Among Workingmen's Families in New York City" (Columbia University, 1909) is illustrative of the influence of the convergence of social statistics and social work, a trend inaugurated by Robert Hunter's work, *Poverty*, in 1904. George Byron Lewis Arner's "Consanguineous Marriages in the American Population" (Columbia University, 1908), reflects the interest in eugenics during the Progressive Era. For a discussion of the role of the eugenics movement in the social sciences during the

Progressive Era, see Mark H. Haller's *Eugenics: Hereditarian Attitudes in American Thought* (New Brunswick, New Jersey: Rutgers University Press, 1963), pp. 21-75. Finally, Donald Mitchell Marvin's dissertation, "Occupational Propinquity as a Factor in Marriage Selection" (University of Pennsylvania, 1918), is a harbinger of the empirical research into mate selection which would characterize much family study in the late 1920s and 1930s.

11. These observations are based upon an examination of the following texts, which exclusively dealt with the family: Helen Bosanquet, *The Family* (London: Macmillan and Company, 1906); James Quayle Dealey, *The Family in Its Sociological Aspects* (Cambridge, Massachusetts: Houghton Mifflin Company, Riverside Press, 1912); John M. Gillette, *The Family and Society* (Chicago: A. C. McClurg and Company, 1914); Willystine Goodsell, *A History of the Family as a Social and Educational Institution* (New York: Macmillan Company, 1915); Frank N. Hagar, *The American Family: A Sociological Problem* (New York: University Publishing Society, 1905); and Elsie Clew Parsons, *The Family: An Ethnographical and Historical Outline with Descriptive Notes, Planned as a Text-book for the Use of College Lecturers and Directors of Home-reading Clubs* (New York: G. P. Putnam's Sons, Knickerbocker Press, 1906). Helen Bosanquet was the wife of Bernard Bosanquet, an early leader of the charity organization movement in England. Willystine Goodsell was an educator, and most of her career was spent as a faculty member of the Teachers College of Columbia University. Frank N. Hagar was a lawyer. James Quayle Dealey, John M. Gillette, and Elsie Clews Parsons were sociologists. In addition, the following general sociology textbooks were examined for their coverage of the family: Frank W. Blackmar, *The Elements of Sociology* (New York: Macmillan Company, 1905), pp. 99-108; Charles A. Ellwood, *Sociology and Modern Social Problems* (New York: American Book Company, 1913), pp. 76-167; Arthur Fairbanks, *Introduction to Sociology*, 7th ed., rev., and in part rewritten (New York: Charles Scribner's Sons, 1901), pp. 170-85; Edward Carey Hayes, *Introduction to the Study of Sociology*, 6th ed. (New York: D. Appleton and Company, 1918), pp. 525-36; Charles Richmond Henderson, *Social Elements, Institutions, Character, Progress* (New York: Charles Scribner's Sons, 1898), pp. 62-77; Edward Alsworth Ross, *The Principles of Sociology* (New York: Century Company, 1920), pp. 583-90; Albion Small and George E. Vincent, *An Introduction to the Study of Society* (New York: American Book Company, 1894), pp. 241-80; and Carroll D. Wright, *Outline of Practical Sociology*, 5th ed., rev. (New York: Longmans, Green, and Company, 1902), pp. 63-71, 160-222.

12. The social case worker's perspectives of the family as an object of

therapy can most clearly be seen in the writings of Mary Richmond. In particular, see her chapter, "The Family Group," in her *Social Diagnosis* (New York: Russell Sage Foundation, 1917), pp. 134-59. Also see Frank Dekker Watson's book, *The Charity Organization Movement in the United States: A Study in American Philanthropy* (New York: Macmillan Company, 1922), pp. 527-29, and Lubove, *Professional Altruist*, pp. 40-41.

13. This conception of the family is characteristic of the literature written by the sociologists mentioned in footnote 11. Perhaps the clearest and most concise exposition of these views can be found in Gillette, *Family and Society*, pp. 16-25.

14. For a good discussion of the divorce issue in the social sciences, see William L. O'Neill, *Divorce in the Progressive Era* (New Haven, Conn: Yale University Press, 1967), pp. 168-97, or his article, "Divorce and the Professionalization of the Social Scientist," *Journal of the History of the Behavioral Sciences* 2 (1966), 291-302 (hereinafter referred to as *JHBS*) (1966), 291-302.

15. Walter F. Willcox, *The Divorce Problem: A Study in Statistics*, Columbia University Studies in History, Economics, and Public Law, Vol. 1 (New York: Columbia University Press, 1891), p. 73.

16. Ibid., p. 74.

17. The full title of the work is *A History of Matrimonial Institutions Chiefly in England and the United States with an Introductory Analysis of the Literature and the Theories of Primitive Marriage and the Family*, 3 vols. (Chicago: University of Chicago Press, 1904).

18. Ibid., 3: 223-24.

19. Ibid., 3: 226-29. Also see his article, "Is the Freer Granting of Divorce an Evil?" *AJS* 14 (1909): 772-76.

20. *History of Matrimonial Institutions*, 3: 250.

21. Ibid., 3: 235-39.

22. "Social Control and Family Function," *Congress of Arts and Science: Universal Exposition, St. Louis, 1904*, 7 vols. (Cambridge, Mass.: Houghton Mifflin and Company, Riverside Press, 1906), 7: 700.

23. *History of Matrimonial Institutions*, 3: 228-29.

24. Ibid., 3: 229.

25. Ibid., 3: 227.

26. Ibid., 3: 256-58. Also see his "Freer Granting of Divorce," p. 776.

27. Columbia University Studies in History, Economics, and Public Law, Vol. 35 (New York: Columbia University Press, 1909).

28. Ibid., pp. 510-27.

29. Ibid., pp. 548-63.

30. Lichtenberger noted this characteristic of the moral reformers and derogatorily referred to them as "moral alarmists," contrasting them to

"users of inductive methods," among whom were sociologists (ibid., pp. 355-56).

31. Examples of this appear throughout the periodical literature which was surveyed. For details of this survey, see footnote 29 of chapter I. As Lichtenberger noted, the literature of the moral reformers was generated from fixed moral beliefs and was impervious to empirical evidence (see ibid.). As a result, this literature does not have any real chronological development. For example, the note of alarm sounded by Noah Davis in 1884 in his article "Marriage and Divorce" is identical in tone to the alarm sounded by Jesse Hill in his article "A Plea for the Family," *Biblioteca Sacra* 62 (1905): 626-39, over twenty years later.

32. O'Neill, *Divorce in the Progressive Era*, p. 172.

33. Ibid., pp. 174-75.

34. This conception of the League as a bridge between the sociologists and moral reformers periodically appears in the annual reports of Dike's organization. The fullest explication of it can be found in his report for 1908, which was issued in the wake of the stormy debate between the moral reformers and the sociologists that took place at the annual conference of the American Sociological Society that year. "Report of the Corresponding Secretary," *Report of the National League for the Protection of the Family for the Year Ending December 31, 1908* (1909), pp. 14-15 (hereinafter referred to as *NLPF Report*). For the details of the debate between the sociologists and moral reformers see *Papers and Proceedings of the American Sociological Society* 3 (1908): 164-80.

35. "Report of the Corresponding Secretary," *Report of the National Divorce Reform League for the Year Ending December 31, 1893* (1894), p. 9 (hereinafter referred to as the *NDRL Report*).

36. This observation is based upon a reading of virtually everything Dike published during his lifetime and is characteristic of all his writings, with the exception of his early 1881 speech, "Facts as to Divorce in New England."

37. *NLPF Report* (1910), pp. 9-13.

38. *NDRL Report* (1896), p. 21.

39. "The Sociological Treatment of Some American Social Institutions," *AJS* 7 (1901): 409.

40. Ibid., pp. 406-7.

41. Cravens, "Abandonment of Evolutionary Social Theory," pp. 11-13. Also see Maus, *Short History of Sociology*, pp. 97-107.

42. Fairbanks, *Introduction to Sociology*, pp. 179-83.

43. Blackmar, *Elements of Sociology*, pp. 105-6.

44. The full title of this work is *Social Organization: A Study of the Larger Mind* (New York: Charles Scribner's Sons, 1909).

45. Ibid., pp. 28-29.

46. Ibid., pp. 24-26.

47. Cooley noted that settlement house workers had made similar conclusions about the importance of primary groups and had applied them to their work with street gangs. Rather than trying to break them up, settlement house workers developed programs designed to convert street gangs into more constructive "boys clubs." See ibid., pp. 27, 49-50. This ability of settlement house workers to recognize aspects of Cooley's concepts about primary groups may well have been due to their general orientation to philanthropy. Unlike charity organization workers, settlement house workers employed a broader philanthropic perspective, which focused upon the community and neighborhood rather than the family. This perspective is clearly evident in Robert Woods' article, "The Neighborhood and the Nation," *NCCC* 36 (1909): 101-6. Also see Graham Taylor's article, "The Neighborhood and the Municipality," ibid., pp. 156-63.

There is evidence that charity organization workers were aware of some key concepts of social psychology. E. E. Williamson's article, "The Children's Age," *NCCC* 30 (1903): 192-96, in stressing the importance of kindergarten programs for character development saw the development of the child's character in terms of children's play, the essence of which involved the acting of a part or the impersonation of others. This conception is very similar to George Herbert Mead's famous concept of "taking the role of the other." See his *Mind, Self, and Society from the Standpoint of a Social Behaviorist*, ed. by Charles W. Morris (Chicago: University of Chicago Press, 1934), pp. 159-60. More significantly, Helen Bosanquet, in a discussion of the psychology of family life, developed a conception of the family remarkably similar to that emerging at the time in social psychology. See her *Family*, pp. 246-59. In fact, the similarity of some of Bosanquet's ideas in this section to those of Charles Horton Cooley were striking enough to lead Cooley's biographer, Edward C. Jandy, to defend him from the allegation that he might have borrowed some of his concepts from her work. See his *Charles Horton Cooley: His Life and His Social Theory* (New York: Dryden Press, 1942), pp. 179-80. In general, however, charity organization workers, and their professional descendents, social case workers, failed to develop or employ social psychological perspectives or concepts of the family in their work. Mary Richmond, for instance, makes no mention of Cooley, Mead, Ellwood, or any other prominent social psychologist or their ideas in her major work, *Social Diagnosis*. Indeed, Peter Leonard found the absence of social psychology in the field of social work in the first two decades of the twentieth century as one of the major distinctions between sociology and social work during this period. See his *Sociology in Social Work* (London: Routledge and Kegan Paul, 1966), pp. 7-11.

48. *Social Organization*, p. 49. Also see his *Human Nature and the Social Order*, rev. ed. (New York: Charles Scribner's Sons, 1922; reprint ed., New York: Schocken Books, 1964), pp. 416-17.

49. *Social Organization*, p. 49. Also see his *Human Nature and the Social Order*, rev. ed. (New York: Charles Scribner's Sons, 1922; reprint ed., New York: Schocken Books, 1964), pp. 416-07.

50. Ibid., pp. 18-19. This focus upon the fundamental condition of mankind as social interdependence was echoed by Frank Tucker in his presidential address to the National Conference of Charities and Correction in 1913. See his address, "Social Justice," *NCCC* 40 (1913): 12-13. The years immediately preceding and following the national presidential election campaign of 1912 in many ways mark the period of greatest influence of the settlement house movement in the United States. Tucker's address reflects much of the spirit of this movement by the time. Also see Allen F. Davis' *Spearheads for Reform: The Social Settlements and the Progressive Movement, 1890-1914* (New York: Oxford University Press, 1967), pp. 194-221.

51. For a good, concise assessment of Ellwood's influence on social psychology, see Fay Berger Karpf's *American Social Psychology: Its Origins, Development and European Background* (New York: McGraw-Hill Book Company, Inc., 1932), pp. 385-94.

52. O'Neill, *Divorce in the Progressive Era*, pp. 186-90.

53. *Sociology and Modern Social Problems*, pp. 83-85.

54. Ibid., 81-82.

55. Ibid., 158-59, 168-69.

56. Even as late as 1943, Ellwood's views on divorce remained unchanged from the position he held in 1913. See his *Sociology: Principles and Problems* (New York: American Book Company, 1943), pp. 134-63.

57. *Sociology and Modern Social Problems*, pp. 164-65.

58. Ibid., p. 168.

59. The two principal expressions of Ellwood's endeavors to develop a sociologically sophisticated religion are his *Reconstruction of Religion: A Sociological View* (New York: Macmillan Company, 1922), and his *World's Need for Christ*, with a foreword by Samuel McCrea Calvert (New York: Abingdon Cokesbury Press, [c. 1940]).

60. The comments and page references will refer to the second edition, which was printed in 1927. Aside from minor internal reorganization of the material, this edition is identical to the first edition. See the "preface to Second Edition," *The Polish Peasant in Europe and America*, 2 vols. (New York: Alfred A. Knopf, 1927; reprint ed., New York: Dover Publications, Inc., 1958) 1: [xi].

61. This is an understatement. *The Polish Peasant* can be regarded as a

pioneer work in social anthropology, American immigration history, social psychology, and general sociology as readily as it can be classified as a contribution to family sociology. So broad is the scope of the work that, as Robert Faris has noted, its influence has never really been felt as a whole but rather as developments of various aspects of the work. See his *Chicago Sociology*, pp. 17-18. The assessments of *The Polish Peasant* are numerous. Probably the most important is Herbert Blumer's *Critiques of Research in the Social Sciences: I: An Appraisal of Thomas and Znaniecki's The Polish Peasant in Europe and America*, Social Science Research Council Bulletin 44 (New York: Social Science Research Council, 1939). Also see Morris Janowitz's "Introduction," to his edition of *W. I. Thomas on Social Organization and Social Personality* (Chicago: University of Chicago Press, 1966), pp. vii-lviii; Kimball Young, *The Contribution of William Isaac Thomas to Sociology*, reproduced by special arrangement with Sociology and Social Research (Los Angeles?: University of Southern California Press, [1963?]): John Madge, *The Origins of Scientific Sociology* (New York: Free Press, 1962), pp. 52-87; and Harry Elmer Barnes, "William Isaac Thomas: The Fusion of Psychological and Cultural Sociology," Barnes, ed., *Introduction to the History of Sociology*, pp. 793-804.

62. Thomas and Znaniecki went further than simply saying that peasant culture was bound together by primary group relationships. They used this observation to make the generalization that primary-group relationships, involving face-to-face contact and interaction with entire personalities, were characteristic of all human relationships until very recently and that, at the time of their writing, only in "a few large cities scattered over the world [has] the primary group . . . lost its importance." Ibid., 2: 1118.

63. Ibid., 2: 1128.

64. Ibid., 2: 1167-68.

65. Ibid., 1: 94-98, 158-64, 2: 1138.

66. Ibid., 2: 1168, 1174.

67. Ibid., 2: 1120, 1139.

68. Ibid., 2: 1168-69. This concept of interdependence between the family and the community is similar to views developed among settlement house workers. See Woods, "Neighborhood and Nation," pp. 101-2, and Taylor, "Neighborhood and Municipality," pp. 157-58.

69. Ibid., 2: 1169.

70. Ibid., 2: 1117.

71. Ibid., 2: 1117-18.

72. Ibid., 2: 1118-19.

73. Ibid., 1: 1-3.

III

FROM ECOLOGY TO INTERACTION: FAMILY SOCIOLOGY IN THE 1920s AND 1930s

Ronald L. Howard

Following World War I, the transformation of family sociology was profound. During the Progressive Era, sociologists had come to view the family as a strong, if troubled, institution, whose difficulties were tied to the larger problems of social reform. In the 1920s, this perspective was replaced by a newer one, which emphasized the internal processes of interaction and personal adjustment.

This shift in perspective was tied to a number of changes in American society and to internal developments in American sociology. The American economy, for decades dominated by such primary industries as steel and oil, was transformed into an economy led by secondary consumer industries such as the automobile industry. This industrial transformation was linked to profound social changes in American values and institutions. Americans, traditionally encouraged to save and long assured of the virtues of self-denial, were now encouraged to live on credit. Promoting this value transformation, the modern advertising industry emerged in the years immediately after World War I, led by executives who had learned their trade in the War Bond, Red Cross, and church drives in the 1918-1920 period. Developments in the field of communications, radio in particular, aided the efforts of Madison Avenue. The institutions of consumer credit and modern advertising created a new set of values that altered the way Americans viewed themselves and their society. The popular concern for community improvement that characterized the American society before the war was replaced by a new preoccupation with individual self-expression and self-indulgence.

The emergence of these values and attitudes created a new wave of popular concern for the institution of the family. This new concern had two major aspects. First, it renewed popular anxiety about the future of the family, once again seen as threatened by the emergence of values hostile to its preservation. Second, these new values, combined with popular conceptions of Freudian theory and concepts borrowed from child psychology, added a new dimension to the problems of child neglect. Freudian theory and the findings of early child psychologists placed a premium upon the influence of early childhood experiences on the subsequent development of the personality.[1] Social responsibility was no longer seen as a guarantee of successful parenthood. The problems of child neglect, then, were broadened to include children of the prosperous as well as the poor. This new popular concern prompted a public demand for programs of parent education, a demand that sociologists, along with home economists, psychiatrists, child psychologists, doctors, clergymen, social workers, and others, tried to meet.[2]

The clearest example of a sociologist caught up in this public demand for popular education in marriage and family life is Ernest R. Groves (1877-1946). Born and reared in New England, Groves received a Bachelor of Divinity degree from Yale in 1901. Though he never went on to enter the ministry, he wrote and delivered sermons in local churches in order to work his way through divinity school. In 1903 he received a B.A. from Dartmouth and began his teaching career the following year at the University of New Hampshire as an instructor in English and Philosophy. By 1909 he had founded a department of sociology at New Hampshire, which he headed from 1914 to 1920. From 1920 to 1927 he held a chair in sociology at Boston University and in 1927 moved to the University of North Carolina, where he continued his career until his death in 1946.[3]

Groves' interest in the field of psychiatry was his point of entry into the field of family sociology.[4] He was worried about the process of social change and its effects upon the family; he constantly sought for a middle ground between moral conservatives, who opposed changes in the family and its relationship with society, and moral radicals, particularly those who called for the removal of all restrictions upon divorce and advocated the institution of trial marriage.[5] He was interested in the factors that sustained marriages and came to believe that affection, initially based upon sex, but a product of experience and mutual concern as well, was the fundamental quality determining the success or failure of a marriage.[6] The development of affection was not the inevitable result of a prescribed list of moral strictures. It was the eventual product of a process of mutual accommodation and adjustment, one that varied in each individual case.[7] The conditions of modern life had stripped the family of many of its past advantages, and with them the factors that promoted family stability. Under these conditions, the difficulty of developing the sentiment of affection within marriage and family relationships was greatly increased.[8]

For Groves, successful marriage and family life had become an exacting art, one that required deliberate training and education.[9] He dedicated his career to meeting this need. He established the first college-level course in preparation for family life at Boston University in 1924, and he was called to the University of North Carolina to establish a similar course there for senior men. The course proved to be extremely popular. Over the years the course grew, as section after section was added. Eventually he offered the course at Duke University as well.[10] Ultimately, the unscheduled demands made upon his time as a marriage counselor led to the establishment of an annual institute for the training of marriage counselors.[11] Groves' influence, if judged upon the bulk of publications alone, was immense, as he wrote several dozen books and scores of articles.[12] In addition, Groves served as the editor of a section of *Social Forces* on marriage and the family from 1928 until his death in 1946. Under his editorship, the family section of *Social Forces* became a major forum for articles and monographs on marriage and the family, particularly during the late 1920s and 1930s.

The development of popular courses and books in marriage and family adjustment and education paralleled similar developments within the field of sociology, initially set in motion by the writings of Cooley, Mead, Thomas and Znaniecki, and others in the emerging field of social psychology. By the 1920s, this development had renewed sociological interest in the family as an agency socialization and personality development. It rested upon a refinement of the concepts of personality formation initially developed in social psychology as interaction theory.

The concept of interaction, which was to form the heart of the new sociological perspective of the family in the 1920s and 1930s, was elaborately developed in Robert E. Park's (1864-1944) and Ernest W. Burgess' (1886-1966) text, *Introduction to the Science of Sociology*, first published in 1921. Interaction was the essential element of society. Society was a process of mutual influence and adjustment between the individuals and groups that composed it. This view of society provided a fluid and dynamic perspective that was congenial to the social-psychological concepts developed in the previous decades and, like them, presupposed that society was the product of individual and group influence.[13]

Five years later, Ernest W. Burgess applied the concept of interaction to his definition of the family in his article, "The Family as a Unity of Interacting Personalities."[14] This article became the cornerstone of family sociology in the 1920s and 1930s.[15] It provided the foundation for the new sociological perspective of the family developed in these decades. Burgess suggested that the family, like society, was essentially a process, one that changed with time and whose essential nature was both created and influenced by the individuals within it.[16] This conception of the family provided sociologists with a functional explanation of their previously developed belief that the family was a strong and flexible institution. The family was strong and flexible because its essential quality lay within the interaction of its members with each other, rather than in its external relations with society. The family continued to live as long as its members continued to interact; it died when its members ceased to interact with each other.[17]

To explain discord and stress, Burgess incorporated into his core concept of the family as interaction the concept of social disorganization developed by Thomas and Znaniecki in *the Polish Peasant*.[18] Interaction occurred not simply between family members as individuals, but between family members as personalities: individuals equipped with status, with self-conceptions of the roles in the family, with an awareness of how their status was viewed by others, and with an awareness of the status and roles of the other family members. Family discord and disorganization resulted from conflicting conceptions of family-member roles. Like George Elliott Howard more than two decades before, Burgess saw family discord and disorganization not as a symptom of family disintegration but as reflection of the conditions of social change. The eventual establishment of a new state of social equilibrium would be accompanied by a stabilization in the patterns of family life.[19]

Burgess suggested that because human interaction generally encompassed a wide variety of behavior, so the family, as a form of human interaction, displayed a wide variety of types. Family types were related to the larger society in different ways, though all shared the common core of interaction. Burgess was impressed with the relative newness of the isolated nuclear family common in urban areas of America. He pointed out that this basic family form was peculiarly adapted to conditions of social change, as it was effectively created anew with each marriage and redefined in the patterns of interaction established between husbands and wives and later between parents and children. By contrast, the larger extended family forms of preindustrial societies were designed to resist social change, as patterns of interaction in these family forms continued as unbroken traditions through family heads and their descendants. Extended families tended to standardize the behavior patterns within them. Nuclear families displayed a wide variety of behavior patterns, which Burgess linked to patterns of human ecology in urban areas. Nuclear family types were related to certain specific urban areas for, as with natural species, the folkways and mores of a local community area provided a specific cultural ecology within which certain family types thrived while others became extinct.[20]

The article's influence was immense, resting not upon the originality of Burgess' insights but upon his ability to define precisely and fuse together a number of separate concepts from a wide variety of sources into a single, theoretical perspective.[21] His article was a stimulus to much subsequent research. His suggestion of a typology of families based upon differences in the patterns of the interaction of its members was employed in a large number of later family studies.[22] He suggested a new approach to problems of family therapy, which defined rehabilitation in terms of achieving a unity in family member role interaction, rather than attempting to impose external criteria of family harmony upon family members.[23] Finally, his core conception of the family as the process of interaction placed a premium upon a research approach based upon the gathering of case studies rather than statistical analysis, for the key to understanding a particular family pattern was a knowledge of its individual growth and development, rather than the measurement of its qualities at a fixed point in time.[24]

Burgess' conception of the family as the development of patterns of family member interaction was extensively employed in the works of his first major student, Ernest R. Mowrer (1895-). His first work of note, *Family Disorganization*, was based upon the hypothesis that the problems of family disorganization, particularly desertion and divorce, could not be seen either as threats to the continued existence of the family or as results of the presence of a certain form of social or environmental evil. Rather, they should be seen as a process of individualization and differentiation of the conceptions of the various family members' roles.[25] The primary cause of this process was a confusion of the two ideals of family life: traditional attitudes that valued the maintenance of family institutions at the expense of individual interests, and more recent attitudes that placed a premium upon the development of individualism.[26] Borrowing from Thomas and Znaniecki, Mowrer suggested that the process of social disorganization they described as afflicting the extended family system of the Polish peasant was applicable to the problems of disorganization in smaller family organizations as well.[27] Using a combination of statistical and case-study techniques, Mowrer developed an ecology of family disorganization in which he related five family types distinguished by particular patterns of familial interaction to various geographic zones in the city of Chicago.[28] His work concluded with a review of the current techniques of handling problems of family adjustment. He found these inadequate as they involved little more than the imposition of a recipe list of marital rules. Effective control of the problems of disorganization would require more research into the processes of family disorganization.[29]

Burgess continued his family sociology research in connection with his second major student, Leonard S. Cottrell, Jr. (1899-), and extended it into a new area, prediction studies. Burgess had been encouraged by the results of a study he had made in 1928 to develop an instrument that could predict those prisoners most likely to become parole violators to see if a similar instrument could be developed to predict successful marriage adjustment.[30] The study was characteristic of Burgess and reflected his desire to make the field of family sociology a more scientific discipline, while at the same time engaging in research that could be of direct benefit in the more practical areas of marriage guidance and counseling.[31]

The object of the study was to devise a questionnaire that could test potential marriage partners to determine their chances for marital success.[32] The study built upon Burgess' conceptions of family interaction, which he mapped out in his 1926 article. Adjustment was defined in terms of the degree to which the attitudes and behavior of the husband and wife tended to support and complement the proper functioning of the personality structures of each other.[33] The research design involved correlating the relative distribution of answers to a series of questions among categories of couples who had previously been classified according to the degree to which they believed their marriage was either happy or unhappy.[34]

The research results tended to reinforce Burgess' assumptions about marriage interaction. Happy marriages were postively associated with homogeneity of interests, age, and educational level. The study reiterated a theme developed earlier by Mowrer—that successful marriages tended to be those based upon the more rational criteria of companionship, or the degree to which couples enjoyed doing things together, rather than the criteria of love at first sight and the disregard of parental wishes. Rather, happy marriages tended to have the blessing and support of parents, were preceded by long engagements, and joined together sociable, outgoing couples who probably lived in single-family dwellings.[35]

Overall, the study indicated that patterns of childhood affection had a direct influence on adult sex and love life, as did childhood socialization. Finally, actual sexual adjustment was as much a matter of biological factors as it was a matter of psychogenetic development and cultural conditioning. Burgess' study augmented a fundamental contention of psychiatry, that childhood experiences did bear a direct relation to subsequent adult adjustment.[36]

Burgess' and Cottrell's study was in a number of ways the most characteristic of family sociology studies during these decades. The problem it was designed to alleviate, marital maladjustment, lay at the heart of the interest of family sociology in the 1920s and 1930s. Its dual goals, to uncover through empirical research underlying factors in family life that could lead to a more coherent conceptualization of marital interaction and to provide a useful tool for family counselors, reflected the tendency of family sociology to reconverge with areas of family social work. Family sociology, along with the field of social work, was moving away from wide-scale programs of social reform and analysis in favor of approaches concerned with individual adjustment.[37] These newer approaches, animated by Burgess' conception of the family as a process of interaction and by similar conceptions of personality development derived from child psychology and social psychiatry, suggested that the phenomena of marriage adjustment, family interaction, and child development were far more complex and interrelated than the simpler perspectives of marriage and the family common to the Progressive Era. Increasingly in the 1920s and 1930s, this perspective nurtured a belief among all students of the family—sociologists and social workers, psychiatrists and marriage counselors, home economists and clergymen—that family study and research required an interdisciplinary approach.[38]

The dominance of this interactional interdisciplinary perspective is effectively demonstrated in the collection of studies that emerged during the 1930s devoted to the effects of the Depression on family life. Their common approach focused upon the techniques of adjustment that families used to cope with the depression. Robert Cooley Angell (1899-), a nephew of Charles Cooley and a professor of sociology at the University of Michigan, directed his attention not to the economic effects of the Depression but to the effects of the Depression upon family interaction patterns.[39] He developed a two-dimensional typology to classify families along axes of integration, or the degree to which the family did things together as a group, and adaptability, or the degree to which families were able to alter their patterns of interaction to straightened circumstances.[40] He used a group of fifty families, all permanent residents of the United States, all with family relations intact (no desertion or divorce), who had suffered at least a twenty-five percent decrease in family income over a long period of time.[41] Angell discovered that adaptability, rather than integration, was the key to survival.[42] Families that tended to act together as a unit but whose interactional roles were rigidly defined survived less well than families whose members tended to engage in individual activities but who were able to readapt their family roles to best meet new circumstances.[43]

Like Angell, Ruth Shonle Cavan (1896-), a sociologist trained at the University of Chicago, and Katherine Howland Ranck (1899-), a psychiatric social worker, made use of case studies as the basis for their research. They converted their research into a longitudinal study by selecting case studies of 100 families who had been referred to the Juvenile Research Institute in Chicago in the years immediately preceding the stock market crash in 1929.[44] They augmented these records with follow-up interviews gathered in 1934 and 1935.[45] The objective of their research was to determine the relationship between family unity and its ability to adjust to the social and economic conditions created by the Depression. Unity was defined by Cavan and Ranck as consensus in family objectives and family ideals, the subordination of personal ambition to family goals, and the degree to which family members found satisfaction of their individual interests within the family group.[46] They discovered that well-organized families with a high degree of unity were more susceptible to the disorganizing effects of the Depression than families with lower degrees of unity, but that they were able to adapt and adjust to the Depression better than families with a low degree of unity.[47] They believed that more extensive analysis of case studies of family adjustment offered the potential of being able to predict the response of families to economic crisis.[48]

A third study, Katherine DuPre Lumpkin's (1897-) *Family: A Study of Member Roles*, was primarily a case study analysis of the process of family member role interaction and adaptation to conditions of stress. Effectually, it was a family sociology study of the effects of the Depression. Forty-six working-class families on relief were analyzed for the condition of stress imposed by unemployment and reduction of family income caused by the Depression. Designed less as a test of a specific research hypothesis than as a demonstration of the use of case-study analysis techniques in family research, the study did not produce clearly defined conclusions. Lumpkin did offer the tentative observation that families organized along democratic lines allowing for some flexibility in authority patterns and family member roles did adapt to the conditions of the depression better than families organized along patriarchal lines.[49]

Finally, Winona Louise Morgan (1907-), in *The Family Meets the Depression*, made use of a follow-up questionnaire and interview survey of 331 families studied in an earlier work by Ruth Lindquist, *The Family in the Present Social Order*.[50] The work by its nature offered descriptions of family life rather than conclusions. Morgan's personal reaction to the survey was surprise at the relatively small degree to which family life in the families surveyed had been adversely affected by the Depression.[51] Straitened circumstances had forced the adoption of a number of economy measures, notably the reduction of social activities and the use of household services such as commercial laundries, but in general had brought no fundamental alteration in family life-styles.[52]

Taken together, these studies illustrate the degree to which the interactionist perspective had come to dominate family sociology by the 1930s. Angell, Lumpkin, Cavan and Ranck, and to a lesser extent Morgan framed their research in terms of internal family adjustment to external crisis; the nature of the crisis itself was incidental. All of them reinforced the traditional sociological image of the family as a strong and adaptable institution. Burgess and Paul L. Schroeder (1894-1966), in summarizing the findings of the Cavan-Ranck study, noted that the family was an excellent institution for adjustment to a crisis.[53] Angell noted that the Depression had produced no apparently sensational impact on family life and concluded that the family had great abilities to resist social changes.[54]

As important as the common perspective and emphasis these
studies placed upon the processes of internal adjustment to external
crisis is the absence of any consideration of the nature of the linkages
of the family to the larger social order. They represent the total
eclipse of the broader community and neighborhood perspective
characteristic of social work and sociology before World War I.
Though these studies explored the problems of family adjustment
at several socioeconomic levels, the comparison of patterns of
family adjustment considered collectively by class or income level
is nonexistent within them. Without much overstatement, these
studies may be said to offer a perspective of American families
during the Depression era as islands of adjustment, floating in an
impersonal social sea.

The interactionist perspective, underpinning the large body of
research in the areas of marital adjustment, parental education,
and patterns of interpersonal interaction and social adjustment,
dominated but did not monopolize the field of family sociology
during the 1920s and 1930s. Two important areas of family research,
one connected with the emerging field of rural sociology and the
other consisting of studies of family patterns in foreign or ethnic
cultures, employed perspectives broader than the intrafamilial level
of analysis characteristic of interactionism.

Within rural sociology, the family was not a major topic of
research interest during the 1920s and 1930s. The reasons for this
lie within the general orientation of rural sociology itself, which
continued to retain a community-wide perspective throughout this
period, much like general sociology during the Progressive Era.
Rural sociology emerged as a distinct field much later than general
sociology, and its development was only beginning by the end of
World War I. Its close association with agricultural departments
and programs of agricultural extension enhanced its distinct orientation toward social problems during these decades. Second, much
of the impetus to the establishment of rural sociology was a reaction
against what its proponents believed was a neglect of rural life. This
factor serves to explain the distinct ethical and ideological flavor of
rural sociology texts during these years. As a result of these influences, the rural sociology textbooks of this period can be described
as a presentation of rural problems combined with a promotion of

the virtues of rural life over urban life.[55] In addition, most rural sociologists entered the field from farm-life backgrounds or careers in agriculture, and their first-hand awareness of the dependency of the farmer on the vagaries of weather, soil, and market conditions favored the development of an ecological rather than an interactional perspective to rural sociological research.[56]

One rural sociologist who did devote much of his research interest to the rural family was Carle C. Zimmerman (1897-). Born in rural Missouri, Zimmerman obtained his B.A. in sociology at the University of Missouri in 1921 and his Ph.D. at the University of Minnesota in 1925. Through the 1920s he held a chair in sociology at the University of Minnesota, moving to Harvard in 1931, where he spent the remainder of his career.[57]

Zimmerman's first major analysis of rural family life appeared as a chapter in a work he coauthored in 1929 with Pitrim Sorokin (1899-1968), *Principles of Rural-Urban Sociology*. This chapter, "The Rural and Urban Family," was a sophisticated comparative analysis of rural and urban family life.[58] It was designed to illustrate the superiority of rural family life, measured in terms of relative prevalence of social pathologies, such as divorce and juvenile delinquency. In an analysis reminiscent of the writings of the moral conservative critics of family life in the nineteenth century, Zimmerman and Sorokin noted that the rural family continued to retain many of the functions its urban counterpart had lost in urban environments, particularly its economic functions. The less-advanced division of labor of rural communities supported the ability of the farm family to continue to operate as an economic unit.[59] Zimmerman and Sorokin tied this attitude to an interactional perspective by noting that the continued function of the rural family as an economic unit promoted a harmony of economic interests among its members that reinforced overall family unity.[60] The economic value of children in rural families tended to keep them under adult supervision longer than was true in urban situations. The absence of alternate social organizations that could serve as primary group substitutes for dissenting adolescents also strengthened parental control.[61] In addition, country life offered fewer temptations such as forms of public entertainment or prostitution.[62] Finally, rural families, by being less geographically mobile, were able to provide a more stable family environment in which to rear children.[63] Only in the area of promoting the development of individualism, and then only when comparing upper-class and upper-middle-class families to rural families organized along patriarchal lines, did Zimmerman and Sorokin concede that urban family life was superior to rural family life.[64]

In 1935, Zimmerman, in collaboration with Merle E. Frampton (1903-), a graduate student in sociology, wrote his main work, *Family and Society*.[65] This study was designed to bring to the attention of the sociological community the works of Frédéric LePlay (1806-1882), a nineteenth century French social analyst, who contended that the condition of a society could be determined by the type of families within it and the manner in which these families utilized their income.[66] Beyond this methodological approach, LePlay offered a hierarchy of three family types: patriarchal families, stem or modified patriarchal families, and individualist or nuclear families.[67] Each of these was associated with a particular stage of social development. Of these three types, the stem family was the form LePlay associated with the highest degree of social stability.[68] As a modification of the extended patriarchal family, the patriarch designated one of his offspring to be the heir of the family estate. The heir continued to live under the same roof as his father and inherited the estate upon his death. The remaining children, in this arrangement, were free to leave the family estate and establish independent families of their own.[69] LePlay believed the stem family form, by offering the advantages of individual development of its children while maintaining a family estate and preserving family traditions, was essential to the continued maintenance of a strong society. Its form offered the adaptability that the rigidly structured patriarchal family lacked, while avoiding the problems of inadequate socialization and the inability to avoid the disorganizing effects of rapid social change associated with the nuclear family.[70]

Zimmerman and Frampton applied LePlay's techniques of analysis to an isolated mountain community in the Ozarks where they believed that the stem family form was most prevalent in an otherwise nuclear-family society.[71] The analysis did not bear out LePlay's contention that family types were invariably associated

with particular forms of larger social organization. They did come
to the conclusion that Ozark family life was superior to that in a
New England mill town with which they compared it.[72] As in the
Zimmerman-Sorokin study, this comparison was made on the basis
of statistics of social pathology and family disorganization. Although
poor and technologically retarded, Ozark family life remained
strong and viable. Zimmerman and Frampton attributed Ozark
family viability to its close interdependence with its larger rural
community.[73] Ozark communities, through the application of
informal community sanctions, were far better able to resolve
problems of crime and the violation of community mores without
breaking up the affected families than were urban families of the
industrial mill town.[74] Finally, the economic effects of the Depression did not touch either Ozark communities or family life there,
while they had had profoundly disruptive effects upon the family
and community life of the New England mill town.

Zimmerman's work, along with the occasional briefer analyses
of rural family life in rural sociology texts, was a revival of the
values of agrarian life of an earlier age. Zimmerman conceived of
rural family life as the moral foundation of society as well as the
human reservoir which replenished the socially disorganized and
infertile ranks of urban society.[75] It provides a sharp contrast to
the work of family sociologists such as Groves and Burgess.

The second area of family sociology outside the interactionist
perspective during the 1920s and 1930s consisted of studies that
viewed family life from a cultural perspective, employing techniques
borrowed from the new practitioners of social anthropology,
particularly Franz Boas (1858-1942), Bronislaw Malinowski (1884-
1942), and their students.[76] The purpose of many of these studies
was to analyse the effects of social change upon patterns of family
life. The family-life patterns most often analyzed were those of
Oriental families, particularly the Chinese and, to a lesser extent,
the Japanese. China and Japan were undergoing rapid social
change during the 1920s and 1930s. This generated much interest
among family sociologists, particularly in such areas as the changing
status of women and the social changes attendant on the breakdown
of extended family patterns. They found Hawaii especially interesting
for its unrestricted racial intermarriage patterns and large number

of ethnic groups. Collectively, these Hawaiian studies reported a general transition from traditional family patterns toward the nuclear family pattern accompanying the process of Westernization. They reflected many of the findings of Thomas and Znaniecki in their study of the Polish peasant. The process of Westernization led to conflicts between an older generation, which held to the social mores of the traditional culture, and the younger generation, caught between the two cultures.

Doris Lorden (1908-), in her study, "The Chinese-Hawaiian Family," noted that early Chinese-Hawaiian marriage patterns reflected the lack of Hawaiian racial prejudice and the absence of Chinese women. When the Chinese immigrants established themselves as a community and imported women from mainland China, they began to segregate themselves and excluded Chinese-Hawaiians from the Chinese community. Eventually, Chinese-Hawaiians came to adopt American marriage patterns.[77]

Andrew W. Lynd's study, "Assimilation in Rural Hawaii," noted a similar pattern among rural Japanese, an initial pioneer stage in which the small, predominantly male Japanese community adopted local familial customs and intermarried with the native population, a second conservative stage in which the equalization of Japanese sex ratios led to a reassertion of Japanese family and community mores, and a final assimilative state, which arrived with the establishment of mandatory high school attendance laws. The American high school became a source of competing authority to the Japanese family and community mores, and in the absence of support from the surrounding society, Japanese community and family mores were slowly replaced by American mores.[78]

Jitsuichi Masuoka's (1903-) article, "The Structure of the Japanese Family in Hawaii," described the mechanism by which Japanese family culture broke down. Japanese traditions were transferred from the grandmother to the grandchildren. Japanese families, as they were established in Hawaii, tended to be two-generation nuclear families. In the absence of the grandparents, Japanese family tradition was effectively broken.[79]

The largest study of Hawaiian family patterns in these decades was Romanzo Adams' (1868-1942) *Interracial Marriage in Hawaii*. While Adams' work was primarily focused upon the absence of racial discrimination in Hawaii, his study did entail an extensive examination of Hawaiian family life and culture. In general, he concluded that racial amalgamation would eventually eliminate any residual problems of racial prejudice; the impetus toward free interracial marriage had proceeded too far to allow any single ethnic group to isolate itself effectively in a community large enough to maintain a viable segregated existence.[80] He concluded that the high divorce rate in Hawaii reflected the social instability of Hawaiian society caused by the large-scale immigration of a variety of ethnic groups. He predicted that the divorce rate would decline with the stabilization of the population.[81] The cause of divorce was not race, but cultural conflict generated by two opposing sets of marital and familial mores and by the absence of any over-riding community authority to subordinate one of the sets to the other.[82] In Hawaii, as in America, successful marriage was ultimately a matter of mutual adjustment. Where neither party in an inter-racial marriage was able to adjust his attitudes sufficiently to accommodate his companion, the failure of the marriage was a foregone conclusion.[83]

The most important examples of the cultural approach to family research during this period dealt not with foreign culture but with American culture—Robert (1892-1970) and Helen (1896-) Lynd's *Middletown and Middletown in Transition*, and E. Franklin Frazier's (1894-1962) studies of black family life, *The Negro Family in Chicago* and *The Negro Family in the United States*.

The Lynd's studies were examples of the direct application of the new techniques of social anthropology to a midwestern community, Muncie, Indiana.[84] Their study did not focus exclusively upon the family but encompassed the entire community and analyzed it as a culture. Family life was considered in the context of the larger community. The portrait of family life provided by Middletown was a relatively bleak one. Using historical data to augment their field research, the Lynds provided a picture of the changes in family life over an approximately thirty-year period. They noted a slow drift toward home ownership and an increasing tendency to marry at a younger age.[85] Romantic sentiments about marriage and the family dominated Middletown culture.[86] They noted the isola-tion of family life, particularly for women, and concluded that happy marriages in Middletown were a rarity.[87] Increasingly however, women, especially working women, were becoming less tolerant of an unsatisfactory marriage and more and more likely to resort to divorce.[88] Their analysis of child-rearing practices in Middletown recorded the progressive decline of parental authority and the emergence of youth culture. The increasing desire of Middletown's children for independence reflected the new influence of movies, while the automobile provided the means to escape parental control.[89] They concluded that the rising domestic discord in Middletown was an example of cultural lag, the inability of cultural mores, particularly those of marriage and family life, to adapt to the increasing pace of technological change.[90]

A decade later, the Lynds returned to Muncie to determine what effects the Depression had wrought on community life. This research became the basis of a second book, *Middletown in Transition*.[91] Their study recorded a continuing development of the family life patterns they observed ten years before. The decline of parental authority had increased. The major sources of parent-child conflict noted in 1925, associated with dating practices and the use of the family car, remained the locus of conflict in 1935.[92] While not enthusiastic advocates, Middletown's people had come to accept divorce as a part of life.[93] The economic dislocations of the Depression had prompted a decline in antagonism toward married women working, but the changes in family life patterns which the presence of a working wife or mother created were only temporarily tolerated, rather than permanently accepted.[94] Overall, they concluded that the Depression had brought about no major change in the family life in Muncie.[95] In an interesting though pessimistic way, *Middletown in Transition* confirmed the basic conclusion of the Angell, Cavan and Ranck, Lumpkin, and Morgan studies. The Depression had not radically altered the patterns of American family life. However, the main pattern of American family life recorded by the Lynds' study was that of increasing generational conflict and declining parental authority.

E. Franklin Frazier employed a variety of analytical techniques in his studies of black family life. His Ph.D. dissertation was largely confined to black families living in Chicago.[96] Frazier's main object in this study, as was the case with Thomas and Znaniecki's *Polish Peasant*, was to study the problems of black assimilation and adjustment to modern American life, using the tools of sociological analysis. Frazier believed that a study that viewed this problem from the perspective of the family offered the most fruitful approach. His dissertation research attracted much interest, and he was encouraged to expand his analysis to a nationwide scale, receiving an initial research grant in 1929 and a second in 1934.[97] The eventual work, *The Negro Family in the United States*, was published in 1939. The study was Frazier's major work and was one of the most significant sociological studies published during these decades. As this work is an expansion of his earlier *Negro Family in Chicago* and incorporated the major findings of that study, the remarks that follow here about Frazier's research generally refer to the later work.

The framework of Frazier's analysis was presented in a historical format, and approximately the first half of this work was devoted to outlining a history of black family life in America. Frazier stressed that, unlike members of other immigrant groups, the black man was stripped of his African culture and heritage.[98] The slave experience left a legacy of a fragmented and unstable family pattern for most black people. While Frazier was quick to emphasize that near-normal family relationships on occasion did develop, the slave's total lack of rights remained the predominant factor shaping black family life in slavery. The auction block and the master's unrestricted ability to take sexual advantage of black women without regard to their status were a continuing reminder of the fragility of the more natural bonds of family affection. Family life was often reduced to nothing more than the nursing relationship between mother and child.[99]

Frazier used his historical analysis of black family life to develop a typology of black family patterns in the United States that emphasized the important role of the mother and grandmother in slavery as the functional sources of family authority and the preservation of family heritage and contrasted slave family life to the more coherent and stable family patterns that emerged among freed blacks and autonomous Indians-black communities.[100] Frazier's recounting of the effects of emancipation is a testament to the strength of the bond of affection; and he devoted some attention to accounts of the efforts of black families and kinsmen, separated by sale or escape, to reunite and reform their shattered relationships.[101] The disorganizing effects of slavery on black family life were exacerbated by migration from rural areas of the South to the urban areas of the North in the late nineteenth and early twentieth centuries. His chapter entitled "Roving Men and Homeless Women" painted a dismal portrait of the distilled end product of this legacy of disorganized family life; individuals totally devoid of kinship sentiment, who had developed totally rational attitudes not only toward their environment but toward people as well. Sex, in the perspective of these individuals, was reduced to a commodity, completely separated from the human sentiments normally associated with it.[102]

The remainder of his work was devoted to a survey analysis of contemporary black family life that tended to confirm many of the findings of Ernest Burgess and other family sociologists employing an interactionist perspective. In support of their research, largely with white middle-class families, Frazier found a direct relationship between family disorganization and juvenile delinquency. Black family disorganization, like that among white families, was a process that reflected the disorienting effects of the sudden transition from a rural to an urban culture.[103] Frazier, using data gathered in the black communities of Chicago and New York's Harlem, developed an ecological model of family disorganization that supported a similar model developed by Mowrer in his work, *Family Disorganization*. Like Mowrer, Frazier discovered a geographic pattern of family disorganization in which the frequency of broken and disorganized families declined as the distance from the core areas of black communities increased.[104]

Frazier's work presented a picture of black family life largely shaped by the external forces of the institution of slavery, the process of urbanization, and racial discrimination. In looking to the future of black family life, Frazier predicted that those families able to preserve family traditions and educate their members would survive the destructive effects of urban life.[105] He was optimistic that the growing occupational similarity between respective members of the black and white communities would tend to break down the caste distinctions separating them and eventually lead to the assimilation of the black into the mainstream of American life.[106]

This group of studies—Zimmerman's, the Lynds', Frazier's, and those of family life in other cultures—together represent a counter-theme to the major area of family research during the 1920s and 1930s that focused upon internal patterns of behavior and adjustment. They retained their primary analytical focus upon the interrelationship between the family and its larger social environment. Excluding the Lynds' work and those studies which dealt with cultures totally outside the United States or its possessions, it is notable that all of them dealt with family life in minority cultures. The several studies dealing with Japanese family life in Hawaii concentrated upon its failure to maintain itself against the inroads of mainland American culture. Frazier's studies of black family life focused upon the disorganizing effects of slavery, the rapid transition from rural to urban life, and the continuing legacy of racial discrimination. Frazier employed Burgess' conceptions of the family as a unity of interacting personalities, but this approach was framed within the larger perspective of black family life in relation to the black community and society at large. The dislocating effects of slavery, racial prejudice, and rapid social mobility, all external to the family, were of crucial importance in Frazier's study; and their essential character in his analysis influenced the patterns of internal family interaction. Finally, Zimmerman and other rural sociologists who dealt with the farm family perceived it as part of a larger rural culture that had been neglected by an increasingly urbanized society. Farm families, too, were part of a minority culture, whose primary problems were not those of internal interaction but those of adjustment to changing external conditions over which the rural family had no control.

By contrast, virtually all of the interactionist studies of the 1920s and 1930s used white middle-class families as the source of their data. These data source choices were deliberately made in the belief that middle-class white American family life represented the normal pattern of family interaction, as well as the basis for projecting an ideal type of family behavior that could be used as a standard to measure family disorganization. Implied in this choice was the belief that cultural homogeneity rather than cultural pluralism was the goal of social progress. For the interactionists, the problems of internal family adjustment were the fundamental and enduring problems of family life. [107] Yet, the Lynds' study pointed out that even white middle-class family life was altered by social changes beyond its control. The introduction of motion pictures into Middletown had provided the basis for developing alternative cultural ideals for the town's youth, while the automobile, introduced at approximately the same time, provided them the means for escaping parental authority.

For the field of family sociology, the 1920s and 1930s was a period of rapid development with two contrasting themes: the family as a system of personal interrelationships and the family as an institution within a larger symbiotic relationship between the community and society. Each theme generated its own methods of research, interaction making use of techniques of case study analysis borrowed from the field of social work, statistics, and the development of questionnaires designed to serve as predictive instruments. The ecological family studies borrowed techniques of descriptive analysis and participant observation from the field of social anthropology. In addition, Zimmerman employed and promoted the perspective and methodology of family budget analysis developed in the nineteenth century by Frédéric LePlay. Finally, the more complex ecological studies such as Frazier's made use of a variety of techniques, including those developed by the interactionists.

Family sociology then, in the 1920s and 1930s, developed beyond a theoretical perspective and became a field of active research, equipped with a specialized methodology. The development of family research elevated the journal article to a position of major importance in the dissemination of hypotheses and research findings. Journal articles provided family sociologists with a forum in which to preview major hypotheses that were later incorporated into books. The main function of the journal, however, was not to preview material to be subsequently incorporated into a book but to present independent research findings, either to confirm or modify earlier hypotheses, or to present particular applicational results of more generalized theories. The journal article became the major medium for cultural family studies, and virtually the exclusive medium for demographic family studies. [108]

The importance of the journal article is reflected in the emergence of the edited collections of articles that appeared during these decades, the most important of which were Edward B. Reuter's and Jessie R. Runner's *Family*, published in 1931, and Ernest R. Groves' and Lee M. Brooks' (1891-1972) reader, *Readings in the Family*, published in 1934.[109] The basic purpose of the essay collections, to present the reader with a collective statement of the current state of the art, testified to the increasing pace of research publication. No longer was there sufficient time for a single writer to assimilate the bulk of current research, translate it into the pages of a textbook, and expect the result to reflect the latest developments in the field. Finally, these essay collections document the interdisciplinary character of the field of family study.[110] All of them drew upon a wide range of sources, and their collections included the work of a variety of family researchers and therapists. Groves' and Brooks' reader, for instance, contained 247 exerpts from a wide variety of sources, including thirty-one selections from evolutionist and social anthropologists, eleven selections from historians, and dozens of selections from sociologists, social workers, popular writers, and psychologists. Of the twenty-four contributors to *The Modern American Family*, nine were sociologists, five were social workers, four were family counselors or parent educators, two were statisticians, and the remaining contributors included an historian, an economist, an educator, and an anthropologist.

In conclusion, the work of family sociologists in the 1920s and 1930s is hard to distinguish from the general range of family studies during this period. Ernest R. Groves' research in the area of family relations is indistinguishable from the efforts, for instance, of Paul Popenoe (1889-), a family counselor and founder of the Institute of Family Relations in Los Angeles.[111] Similarly, the studies of family sociologists employing the methodology of social anthropology resembles the work of the ethnologists themselves. Family sociology came to be an established field within the discipline of sociology during these decades, its official recognition dating from the establishment of a section on marriage and the family at the annual meeting of the American Sociological Society in 1924.[112] At the same time, family sociologists became an intimate part of the general field of family research that emerged at the end of World

War I. The differences between family research and family social work were never very great, and they tended to disappear altogether in the late 1920s and 1930s. It was an era in which empirical research in marriage and the family and the development of therapeutic techniques were closely intertwined. Family sociologists developed a twofold perspective of the family as, on the one hand, a social institution with remarkable powers of adaptation and survival and, on the other, from the standpoint of the individual family and its members, a complex process of developing patterns of interaction and adjustment, whose proper and healthy development was a skilled and demanding art. This twofold perspective would continue to dominate family sociology in the following decade, but the multifaced approach to family research, both anticipated and exemplified by E. Franklin Frazier's work, was to play an increasingly important role as family sociologists attempted to develop a new theoretical approach that could simultaneously account for internal interaction and external family relations.

NOTES

1. J. C. Flugel's *Psycho-Analytic Study of the Family* (6th ed., London: The Hogarth Press, 1939), first published in 1921, was one of the most significant applications of Freudian theory to family interaction and child development. See, in particular, Chapter 5, "The Family and the Growth of Individual Personality," and Chapter 14, "The Attitude of Parents to Children."
2. Floyd Nelson House offers an excellent brief analysis of the influence of psychiatry and child psychology upon sociology and the general public in his work, *The Development of Sociology* (New York: McGraw-Hill Book Co., Inc., 1936), pp. 360-66. Also see Meyer Francis Nimkoff's *Family* (Cambridge, Mass.: The Riverside Press, Houghton-Mifflin Co., 1934), pp. v-vi; and Ernest R. Groves' *The Drifting Home* (Cambridge, Mass.: The Riverside Press, Houghton-Mifflin Co., 1926), pp. 135-53.
3. Details of Groves' life can be found in his obituary by Rupert B. Vance in *American Sociological Review* 11 (1946): 754-55 (hereinafter referred to as *ASR*), and Howard W. Odum's article, "Ernest R. Groves and His Work," *Social Forces* 25 (1946): 197-206.
4. See Vance, "Groves," p. 755. Groves' interest in psychiatry is evident in his early rural sociology text, *The Rural Mind and Social Welfare* (Chicago: University of Chicago Press, 1922), pp. 86-107, although he

made use of William McDougall's instinct psychology in this work, he quickly repudiated this approach.

5. Groves' concern about the effects of social change upon the family can be found in his earliest work. See, for instance, his *Rural Problems of Today* (New York: Association Press, 1918), pp. 5-23. Groves' analysis of the family and its problems was couched within a framework of moral judgments about family life which emphasized an ideal family as rural, middle-class, and living in a single-family dwelling. This is clearly evident in his work cited here. His attack against the advocates of trial marriage centered upon his belief that such relationships too exclusively focused upon sexual attraction and formed the central thesis of his book, *The Marriage Crisis* (New York: Longmans, Green, and Co., 1928). See, in particular, Chapter 6, "Shall We Make Marriage Experimental?" On the other hand, he saw sex in a positive rather than a negative light and strongly opposed ascetic or repressive solutions to marriage problems (*Marriage Crisis*, pp. 212-14, 220-21).

6. This idea is a recurrent theme in Groves' writings. See, for instance, his textbook, *Marriage* (New York: Henry Holt and Co., 1933), p. 6; his *Marriage Crisis*, pp. 66-71; and his *Social Problems of the Family* (Philadelphia: J. B. Lippincott Co., 1927), pp. 58-59.

7. *Social Problems of the Family*, pp. 194-96.

8. This idea recurs throughout his work; see, for instance, his *Rural Problems of Today*, pp. 5-7, 18-19; *Marriage Crisis*, pp. 46-50; *Social Problems of the Family*. This theme of declining family functions was independently advanced by William Fielding Ogburn. Like Groves, he concluded that the bond of affection was the primary element determining the success or failure of family life. See his article, "Social Heritage and the Family," in Margaret E. Rich, ed., *Family Life Today: Papers Presented at a Conference in Celebration of the Fiftieth Anniversary of Family Social Work in America Held at Buffalo*, October 2-5, 1927 (Cambridge, Mass.: the Riverside Press, Houghton-Mifflin Co., 1928), pp. 24-39.

9. See his article, "Social Influences Affecting Home Life," *AJS* 31 (1925): 236-37. This article provides the best condensed presentation of Groves' most important ideas. Also see his *Marriage Crisis*, pp. 182, 192, 196-97, 212-15; and his *Drifting Home*, pp. 1-14.

10. Vance, "Groves," p. 755.

11. See Groves' *Marriage Crisis*, pp. 202-03, and Vance, "Groves," p. 755.

12. Odum's article, "Ernest R. Groves and His Work," provides a fairly complete bibliography of his work (pp. 202-06).

13. *Introduction to the Science of Sociology: Including the Original*

Index to Basic Sociological Concepts 3rd ed., rev., with an introduction by Morris Janowitz (Chicago, University of Chicago Press, 1969), pp. 339-46.

14. This article initially was delivered as a paper to the American Sociological Society in December 1925 and was published in *The Family* 8 (1926): 3-9.

15. For an assessment of the influence of this article on family sociology, see Leonard S. Cottrell, Jr.'s "Ernest Watson Burgess, 1886-1966: Contributions in the Field of Marriage and the Family," *Journal of Marriage and the Family* 30 (1968): 6-11.

16. "The Family as a Unity," p. 3.

17. Ibid., p. 5.

18. William Isaac Thomas and Florian Znaniecki, *The Polish Peasant in Europe and America*, 2 vols. (New York: Alfred A. Knopf, 1927; reprint ed., New York: Dover Publications, 1958), 2: 1128.

19. "The Family as a Unity," p. 6.

20. Ibid., pp. 4-5.

21. Cottrell, "Burgess," p. 8.

22. Among the more important of such studies are Robert Cooley Angell, *The Family Encounters the Depression* (New York: Charles Scribners Sons, 1936), and Katharine DuPre Lumpkin, *The Family: A Study of Member Roles* (Chapel Hill, N. C.: The University of North Carolina Press, 1933). Burgess credits the concept of the relation of family types to specific urban areas to Ernest R. Mowrer, "The Family as a Unity," p. 4. Cottrell, however, points out that Burgess had been interested in this idea for some time; see his "Ernest W. Burgess," pp. 6-7. It is certain that the idea of geographically mapping the distribution of social phenomena was a very early activity at the University of Chicago: Burgess himself notes that this phase of research activity was carried on at the University of Chicago from 1916 through the 1920s. See his essay, "A Short History of Urban Research," in *Contributions to Urban Sociology*, edited by Burgess and Donald J. Bogue (Chicago, University of Chicago Press, 1964), pp. 5-7. Also see Mowrer's *Family Disorganization* (Chicago: University of Chicago Press, 1927), pp. 109-23. This ecological concept of family typology was subsequently employed by E. Franklin Frazier in his works, *The Negro Family in Chicago* (Chicago, University of Chicago Press, 1932) and *The Negro Family in the United States* (Chicago: University of Chicago Press, 1939).

23. I am not suggesting that Burgess' interactional idea alone influenced the areas of marriage and family counseling, rather that Burgess' article brought attention to the potential usefulness of interactional concepts in these fields. The interactional approach to family counseling is hinted at in

Thomas and Zaniecki's criticism of the traditional ordering and forbidding form of social control in their "Methodological Note." See *The Polish Peasant*, 1: 3-4. Similar ideas can be found in Ernest R. Groves writing; see in particular, his chapter, "Family Adjustment in his *Social Problems of the Family*, pp. 194-213.

24. Burgess developed this idea most clearly in another essay, "The Family and the Person," which appeared in his edited collection of essays, *Personality and the Social Group* (Chicago: University of Chicago Press, 1929), pp. 123-29. On the other hand, Burgess' advocacy of the usefulness of case histories (an idea that initially had been advanced and extensively applied by Thomas and Znaniecki in *The Polish Peasant*) did not preclude his interest in statistical techniques, as his subsequent work in the development of marriage prediction studies testifies. His familiarity and understanding of both techniques is evident in his article, "Statistics and Case Studies," *Sociology and Social Research* 12 (1927): 103-20.

25. *Family Disorganization: An Introduction to a Sociological Analysis*, p. 4.

26. This idea is extensively developed in his chapter, "Social Forces in Family Disorganization," ibid., pp. 145-73. Groves too expressed similar concepts in his work. See, in particular, his chapter "The Cause of the Marriage Crisis," in his *Marriage Crisis*, pp. 27-46. In general, this idea is strikingly similar to the complaints of nineteenth-century moral conservatives against the rise of "excessive individualism" as a cause of divorce. What separates Groves and Mowrer from the moral conservatives is their reaction to the observation. While the general response of the moral conservatives to excessive individualism was to advocate either the restriction or abolition of divorce, Groves and Mowrer believed the solution to be a matter of education and counseling.

27. *Family Disorganization*, pp. 270-71.

28. Ibid., pp. 109-23.

29. Ibid., pp. 267-89.

30. Ernest W. Burgess and Leonard S. Cottrell, Jr., *Predicting Success or Failure in Marriage* (New York: Prentice-Hall, Inc., 1939), p. ix.

31. Cottrell, "Ernest W. Burgess," p. 11. The continued reliance on Cottrell's article is a reflection of the absence of much personal information about Ernest W. Burgess. While he left his papers to the University of Chicago Library, it is evident from my personal examination of them that virtually all correspondence of a personal nature has been carefully culled out from the scores of boxes containing his papers. A personal conversation I had with Professor Cottrell in June 1974 confirmed this deliberate attempt to remove Burgess' private life from his academic papers. Pro-

fessor Cottrell noted that Burgess, while friendly and helpful, maintained a relatively reserved and formal air about himself, which conveyed the impression that time spent in conversation with him was time being taken from some other important activity or research. The volume of his surviving papers is a testament to Burgess' phenomenal productivity and scholarly research and suggests a tireless, dawn-to-dusk work day. Research was Burgess' life; Professor Cottrell noted that the only time Burgess ever lost his reserve and became genuinely excited was during seminars when students presented research proposals.

32. Burgess and Cottrell, *Predicting Success or Failure in Marriage*, pp. 15, 17-20.

33. This is the definition from the preliminary study by Burgess and Cottrell, "The Prediction of Adjustment in Marriage," *AJS* 1 (1936): 739. In the full version, the definition was simplified to a definition of the degree to which the behavior patterns of the married couple was mutually satisfying, *Predicting Success or Failure in Marriage*, p. 47.

34. *Predicting Success or Failure in Marriage*, pp. 58-74.

35. Ibid., 159-71.

36. Ibid., 341-49.

37. See Peter Leonard, *Sociology in Social Work* (London: Routledge and Kegan Paul, 1966), p. 10, and Roy Lubove, *The Professional Altruist: The Emergence of Social Work as a Career, 1880-1930* (Cambridge, Mass.: Harvard University Press), pp. 55-117.

38. This theme is made explicit by Margaret E. Rich, editor of *Family Life Today*, in her "Preface," pp. v-vi. Indeed, as the title suggests, the work itself is a testament to this idea.

39. *The Family Encounters the Depression* (New York: Charles Scribner's Sons, 1936), p. 4.

40. Ibid., pp. 14-15.

41. Ibid., pp. 4-5.

42. Ibid., p. 114.

43. Ibid., pp. 145-46, 260-62.

44. *The Family and the Depression* (Chicago: University of Chicago Press, 1938), p. 12.

45. Ibid., p. 14.

46. Ibid., p. 3.

47. Ibid., pp. 110-11, 147-49.

48. Ibid., pp. 145-46.

49. (Chapel Hill: University of North Carolina Press, 1933), pp. 166-69.

50. The full title of Morgan's work is *The Family Meets the Depression: A Study of a Group of Highly Selected Families* (Minneapolis: University

of Minnesota Press, 1939). The full title of Lindquist's work is *The Family in the Present Social Order: A Study of Needs of American Families* (Chapel Hill: University of North Carolina Press, 1931). The intimate relationship of family sociology to outside fields is nicely illustrated by these two studies. Linquist's study, while written and published with the cooperation of the American Home Economics Association, was supervised by Ernest R. Groves, a sociologist. See the "Preface." Morgan's follow-up study was a sociology dissertation.

51. Morgan, *Family Meets the Depression*, p. 99.

52. Ibid., pp. 100-101.

53. Cavan and Ranck, *Family and the Depression*, pp. xii-xiii.

54. Angell, *Family Encounters the Depression*, p. 2.

55. These impressions about the treatment of the family in rural sociology textbooks during these decades was derived from the following: John Phelan, ed., *Readings in Rural Sociology* (New York: Macmillan Co., 1920), pp. 162-84, 313-36; Horace Boies Hawthorn: *The Sociology of Rural Life* (New York: The Century Company, 1926), pp. 280-81; John Morris Gillette, *Rural Sociology* (New York: The Macmillan Company, 1923), pp. 367-400; Carl C. Taylor, *Rural Sociology: A Study of Social Problems* (New York: Harper and Brothers, 1926), pp. 186-211; and J[ohn] H[arrison] Kolb and Edmund DeS. Brunner, *A Study of Rural Sociology: Its Organization and Changes* (Cambridge, Mass.: The Riverside Press, Houghton-Mifflin Company, 1935), pp. 17-43. The latter work and three others written at the end of the decade and published in 1940, Paul H. Landis' *Rural Life in Process* (New York: McGraw-Hill Book Co., Inc., 1940), pp. 335-53; Newell LeRoy Sims' *Elements of Rural Sociology* (New York: Thomas Y. Crowell Co., 1940), pp. 498-516; and T. Lynn Smith's *Sociology of Rural Life* (New York: Harper and Brothers, 1940), pp. 350-66, depict a trend away from rural social problems and toward more sophisticated descriptive analyses of rural family life.

56. The most comprehensive history of rural sociology is Lowry Nelson's *Rural Sociology: Its Origin and Growth in the United States* (Minneaspolis: University of Minnesota Press, 1969). This work, however, tends to equate the history of rural sociology with the biographies of its major figures, an approach which limits its usefulness. A useful contemporary analysis of rural sociology is Carle C. Zimmerman's article, "The Trend of Rural Sociology," in George A. Lundberg, Read Bain, and Nels Anderson, eds., *Trends in American Sociology* (New York: Harper and Brothers, 1929), pp. 221-60.

57. Nelson, *Rural Sociology*, pp. 179-82.

58. (New York: Henry Holt and Company), pp. 333-69.

59. Ibid., pp. 347-48.
60. Ibid., p. 348.
61. Ibid., pp. 348-49.
62. Ibid., pp. 349-50.
63. Ibid., pp. 350-51.
64. Ibid., p. 369.
65. The full title of this work is *Family and Society: A Study of the Sociology of Reconstruction* (New York: D. Van Norstrand Co., 1935).
66. Ibid., pp. 85-96.
67. Ibid., pp. 97-102.
68. Ibid., p. 99.
69. Ibid., p. 125.
70. Ibid., pp. 133-34.
71. More precisely, Zimmerman and Frampton selected that area of the United States they believed most likely to be populated by autonomous, self-sustaining, subsistence agricultural families living in autonomous communities isolated from outside influences. These were the conditions which LePlay associated with stem-family patterns. Ibid., pp. 162-63, 170, 141-45.
72. Ibid., pp. 284-86, 353-57.
73. Ibid., pp. 275-84.
74. Ibid., pp. 270-71.
75. Zimmerman went on to expand his application of LePlay's theories into a universal model of the rise and fall of civilization correlated to the general health of family life within it; when family life broke down, so did civilization. It is strikingly similar to arguments developed by moral conservatives in the nineteenth century, and like them, he viewed contemporary family life with considerable alarm. See his article, "The Social Conscience and the Family," *AJS* 52 (1946): 263-67, and his book *The Family of Tomorrow* (New York: Harper and Brothers, 1949).
76. For an excellent discussion of Franz Boas and his influence in transforming anthropology from a speculative discipline into an empirical enterprise, see Mellvill J. Herskovits' biography, *Franz Boas* (New York: Charles Scribner's Sons, 1953), particularly Chapter 2, "Man the Culture-Building Animal," pp. 46-52. Also see H. R. Hays' *From Ape to Angel: An Informal History of Social Anthropology* (New York: Alfred A. Knopf, 1958), pp. 227-35, 256-68.
77. *AJS* 40 (1935): 453-63.
78. *AJS* 45 (1939): 200-14.
79. *AJS* 46 (1941): 168-78. Although this article was published in 1941, Masuoka's findings were based on studies of the Japanese family in Hawaii

made during the 1930s, which came to similar, though not as sharply defined, conclusions. See his "Changing Moral Bases of the Japanese Family in Hawaii," *Sociology and Social Research* 21 (1936): 158-69 (hereinafter referred to as *S & SR*) and his "Japanese Patriarch in Hawaii," *Social Forces* 17 (1938): 240-48 (hereinafter referred to as *SF*).

80. *Interracial Marriage in Hawaii: A Study of Mutually-Conditioned Processes of Acculturation and Assimilation*, p. 13.

81. Ibid., p. 203.

82. Ibid., p. 225.

83. Ibid., p. 226.

84. Robert S. Lynd and Helen Merrill Lynd, *Middletown: A Study of Contemporary American Culture* (New York: Harcourt, Brace, and Company, 1929). Although in the most precise sense, this study is a work of social anthropology, its importance and the strategic selection of its topic has, like *The Polish Peasant*, become an integral part of the literature of anthropology, sociology, and, more recently, history. Therefore, it is important to consider it here.

85. Ibid., pp. 109-11.

86. Ibid., pp. 114-15.

87. Ibid., pp. 120, 130.

88. Ibid., pp. 126-29.

89. Ibid., pp. 131-42.

90. Ibid., pp. 176-78.

91. The full title of this work is *Middletown in Transition: A Study in Cultural Conflicts* (New York: Harcourt, Brace and Company, 1937).

92. Ibid., pp. 168-74.

93. Ibid., pp. 160-62.

94. Ibid., pp. 177, 184-86.

95. Ibid., p. 201.

96. *The Negro Family in Chicago* (Chicago: University of Chicago Press, 1932).

97. *The Negro Family in the United States* (Chicago: University of Chicago Press, 1939), p. xix.

98. Ibid., pp. 21-22.

99. Although diffused throughout the first half of the work, these ideas are most clearly developed in the chapter, "Human, All Too Human," ibid., pp. 21-41. The following chapter, "Motherhood in Bondage," pp. 42-61, developed Frazier's thesis that the fundamental family bond for the black slave was that of the mother to her children.

100. See, in particular, Part II, "In the House of the Mother," and Part

III, "In the House of the Father," ibid., pp. 89-267. Also see his article, "Traditions and Patterns of Negro Family Life in the United States," *Race and Culture Contacts*, Edward Byron Reuter, ed. (New York: McGraw-Hill Book Co., 1934), pp. 191-208.

101. In particular, see Chapter 9, "The Downfall of the Matriarchate," *Negro Family in the United States*, pp. 163-81.

102. Ibid., pp. 271-90.

103. Ibid., pp. 358-75, particularly, pp. 374-75.

104. Ibid., pp. 302-07, 315-18. Also see footnote 28.

105. Ibid., pp. 487-88.

106. Ibid., p. 488.

107. I do not want to suggest an organized conspiracy among the interactionists to flaunt the values and patterns of middle-class white family life over alternative forms. Rather, this pattern is a benign reflection of the white middle-class backgrounds of the interactionists themselves, and the predominance of white middle-class families in the case records used in their studies. If the interactionist group did have an ideologue, it would be Ernest R. Groves. See his essay, "Grinding Down the Middle-Class," in his work *The Drifting Home*, pp. 94-101. Certainly, Groves firmly believed that the fundamental family problems were those of interpersonal adjustment. Professor Rupert Vance, a close associate of Groves at the University of North Carolina, indicated in a conversation I had with him in June 1974 that Groves was antagonistic to the New Deal, believing that environmental and social reform would not solve the fundamental problems afflicting family life.

108. The notable exception to this observation about demographic family studies was Ernest R. Groves' and William Fielding Ogburn's textbook, *American Marriage and Family Relationships* (New York: Henry Holt and Company, 1928), which combined Groves' interactionist analysis of the problems of marriage and family adjustment with Ogburn's extensive demographic survey of American family and marriage patterns.

109. The full title of Reuter and Runner's collection is *The Family: Source Materials for the Study of Family and Personality* (New York: McGraw-Hill Book Company, 1931). Groves' and Brooks' collection was published by J. B. Lippincott Company in Chicago.

110. Reuter's and Runner's and Groves' and Brooks' essay collections should be distinguished from essay collections composed specifically of articles written particularly for that collection, such as Margaret E. Rich's *Family Life Today*, or Donald Young's edition, *The Modern American Family, Annals of the American Academy of Political and Social Science*

160 (March 1932) (hereinafter referred to as *Annals*). Still, all four of these essay collections are characterized by their multidisciplinary approach to the family and its problems.

111. Popenoe, trained as a biologist, entered the family and marriage counseling field through his advocacy of eugenics. Popenoe was a frequent contributor to sociological journals during this period. Burgess and Cottrell's study was also very similar to research in psychology and psychiatry during this period. Note, in particular, Louis M. Terman's work *Psychological Factors in Marital Happiness* (New York: McGraw-Hill Book Co., Inc., 1938), Katharine B. Davis' *Factors in the Sex Life of Twenty-Two Hundred Women* (New York: Harper and Brothers, 1929), and Gilbert V. Hamilton's *Research in Marriage* (New York: A & C Boni, 1929). What distinguished Burgess' and Cottrell's study from these other works was their attempt to develop a predictive instrument, rather than simply to isolate factors either promoting or inhibiting marital adjustment.

112. See Mrs. W. F. Dummer's "Report of the Meeting of the Section of the Family," *Proceedings of the American Sociological Society* 20 (1925): 275-76. The main paper delivered at this first session was Groves' "Social Influences Affecting Family Life," later published in *AJS* as "Social Influences Affecting Home Life." See footnote 9.

IV

EARLY FAMILY SOCIOLOGY IN EUROPE: PARALLELS TO THE UNITED STATES

Louis Th. van Leeuwen _____

INTRODUCTION

During the 1950s and most of the 1960s American family scholars showed a preference for the study and analysis of the family as a small group. This preference can be seen as a result of the intellectual tradition formed during the 1920s and 1930s. When Reuben Hill and John Mogey set out to discover international trends in family research, they found that family scholars outside the United States were less interested in the analysis of the family as a small group. As appears from their trend reports, scholars in regions or nations outside the United States tended to be more interested in macroscopic family studies and in the analysis of transactions between the family and other societal institutions.[1]

Partially, this difference can be explained by the concentration of the activities of cultural anthropologists in regions outside the United States. In addition, one can wonder to what extent intellectual traditions have played a part in producing this difference. This chapter aims at exploring this line of thought with respect to Europe. Using Howard's analysis as a starting point, this chapter systematically compares the history of American and European family research prior to 1940.[2]

Parallels and differences with regard to research themes, theoretical frames of reference, and research strategies are at the core of this comparison. The value orientation of family scholars on both continents is another important element. Dealing with value orientations makes it necessary to pay some attention to the societal context in which family research in both continents developed. In this chapter, I follow the periods used in previous chapters by Howard. The first section deals with the nineteenth century and thus covers roughly the same period as chapter one. The second section of this chapter discusses developments between about 1900 and 1940, and in a way overlaps most of the period Howard discusses in chapters II and III.

NINETEENTH-CENTURY FAMILY STUDIES

From Howard's discussion, the period 1865-1890 appears as one in which family research, as an activity of specialists with an academic or social identity of their own, hardly exists. Judged by the publications and authors Howard discusses for this period, family research is an integral part of activities with a different social or academic identity. Concerned as they were with poverty and other consequences of industrialization and urbanization in nineteenth-century America, moral reformers, social reformers, and charity workers developed a vivid and intense interest in the family. However, neither the reformers nor the charity workers saw themselves, nor were they seen by others, as family researchers. As far as early sociology is concerned, for most sociologists the family was only one of the several institutions they were interested in. To some extent the same situation existed in nineteenth-century Europe. As in the United States the first contributions to family research and family theory can be found either in the more general works of sociologists or in the context of the varied set of activities aimed at the solution of the poverty problem.

Poverty and Empirical Research

Without doubt England has the longest tradition in the collection of empirical data on poverty. From the eighteenth century on, when poverty was still mainly rural and not an urban-industrial problem, individuals, private organizations, government agencies, and parliamentary committees collected empirical data on the poor and their families. By 1845, such data enabled Engels to publish his book *Die Lage der arbeitenden Klassen in England* ("The position of the working classes in England"). Using existing data, Engels discussed the consequences of the shift from cottage industry to production in modern factories for the family life and living conditions of the labourers. Later on, during the nineteenth and the beginning of the twentieth century, Booth and Rowntree did their empirical studies on poverty.[3]

In fact, Rowntree first formulated the idea that the economic situation of the family changed regularly during its life cycle. His data led him to the conclusion that there were two relatively affluent and two relatively stressful financial periods in the family life cycle. During the first years of marriage financial conditions tend to be relatively favorable. The birth of children, however, is the beginning of a period in which financial conditions may become tight. This period ends when children start work and are able to contribute to the family income. The second and last financially difficult period begins when the children have left the parental home to start their own families and the parents are too old to provide for themselves. Rowntree's ideas on the life cycle of the family influenced rural sociologists and home economists in the United States during the 1920s and 1930s and can also be found in the set of ideas that formed the starting point for theories using the conceptual framework of family development in American family sociology after World War II.

Booth and Rowntree were not exceptions to their period. During the second half of the nineteenth century several European scholars showed an interest in empirical budget studies. In France, Frédéric LePlay with his systematic collection of data on the budgets of individual families set an important example. The Belgian statistician Quetelet compared LePlay's budget studies to "a string of separate pearls" and suggested the use of these systematically collected data as a basis for generalizations. Pursuing this line of action, the German economist and statistician Ernst Engel (1821-1896) formulated his well-known economic law, which states that the poorer a family is, the larger will be the proportion of its budget spent on food.[4]

How vivid the interest in the family budget was can be seen from the fact that by the end of the nineteenth century government agencies in several western European countries started to collect and publish family budget data on a regular basis. This development was an integral part of a general rise in interest for the collection, publication, and analysis of several kinds of statistical data. During the second half of the nineteenth century, most of these countries published, or started to publish, statistical data on marriage, births, deaths, suicide, criminality, illegitimacy, and several other social conditions. During this period, a group of German philosophists and philosophers used these data as an indicator for the moral well-being of their nation. One of these so-called *moralstatistiker* ("statisticians of morality") was Alexander Von Oettingen.[5] Moreover, this kind of statistical data enabled Durkheim to do his magnificient study on suicide. Last but not least, available statistical data did lead to a considerable number of demographic publications.

To some extent this growing interest in the collection and publication of statistical data can be explained by the development of government agencies into modern bureaucracies. In that type of organization statistical data both served administrative purposes and functioned as a basis for rational decision-making. Equally important was the changing approach in public life to social issues. Both private persons and organizations showed an increasing interest in the collection and analysis of empirical data on social conditions as a basis for discussion, policy formulation, and action. As discussed previously, in England this trend began at an early date and led to the impressive studies of Booth and Rowntree. For Germany and the Netherlands, two interesting organizations must be mentioned. One is the German *Verein fuer Sozial Politik* ("Association for social policy") that was formed in 1873.[6] Many members of this organization were economists with a strong interest in problems on the borderline between economics, sociology, and politics. The collection of empirical information on actual social and political problems was an important activity of this organization for socioeconomic policy. During the second half of the nineteenth century and the beginning of the twentieth century, they carried out several studies of the poverty problem. One of the specific topics in these studies was labor by women and children.

The second organization is the Dutch *Vereniging voor Statistiek* ("Statistical Association"), founded in 1856. This voluntary association was a meeting point for those interested in the collection publication, analysis, and practical use of statistical data. Among its most influential and active members were several economists with roughly the same line of interest as their colleagues in the German *Verein fuer Sozial Politik*. The *Vereniging voor Statistiek* proved to be very effective in its efforts to stimulate the collection and publication of statistical data by Dutch government agencies. Consequently, by the end of the nineteenth century, the Netherlands had a rather elaborate system of statistical publications. One of the important themes covered by these publications was the working and living conditions of the laboring class.[7]

Despite all these nineteenth-century activities aimed at the collection of empirical data on societal conditions, it must be stated that the motivation for these activities was more often pragmatic than scientific. As far as scientific motives were of importance, economists and statisticians played the dominant role. Sociologists were rarely engaged in these activities. Primarily pragmatic, most of these activities were concentrated on the severe poverty that accompanied Europe's industrialization. The family as such was hardly an objective of study. This, however, does not imply that the studies on poverty and the activities of demographers during this period did not produce any family data at all. In fact, the activities discussed here produced a huge amount of empirical data on families that still awaits analysis by historians and family sociologists. This pragmatically motivated data-gathering on societal conditions is one of the sources to examine for family research and family theories during the nineteenth century. The second main source is sociology.

Nineteenth-century sociology

The development of sociology during the nineteenth century must be seen in the perspective of deep societal changes following the French Revolution and the Industrial Revolution. The developing science of sociology claimed that it could make a new contribution to the philosophical, theological, and political debate about these changes. Instead of the a priori approach of philosophy and theology to societal problems, sociology offered the possibility of a scientific analysis of society and its problems. In these circumstances, it can be understood that social change is the dominant theme of nineteenth-century sociology. Dealing with this theme, most sociologists developed a broad historical perspective on society and its main institutions. One of the institutions most sociologists covered in their macroscopic studies was the family.

The development of theories and concepts played an important part in nineteenth-century sociology. In developing their theories and concepts, most sociologists followed the strategy of desk or library research. Empirical research was a rare exception during this period. Empirical evidence gathered through library research more often functioned as illustration than as proof of theories. Finally, most, if not all, nineteenth-century sociologists did not restrict themselves to a scientific analysis of the problems they addressed. Scientific analysis, moral evaluations, and political recommendations all tended to be intertwined in their work.

Evolutionism

Because a discussion of the family theories of all early European sociologists would go far beyond the scope of this chapter, a selection must be made.[8] Two criteria were used in making this selection. One is to represent the diversity of European sociology, and the second is to show the influence of sociologists and their theories on later development. As in early American sociology, evolutionism played an important part in nineteenth-century European sociology. A considerable number of sociologists during this period were either evolutionist or more or less intensively influenced by evolutionism. Because Howard, in his first chapter, has already paid attention to European evolutionism and its family theories, a further discussion of their contribution is unnecessary here. Some remarks about their influence on public thinking must, however, be made.

From their ideas on social change, evolutionists took a position that opposed traditional thinking about social order as a stable, God-given phenomenon, anchored in natural law. Most evolutionists took the position that evolution and thus social change were synonymous with progress. But in their conception of progress, most evolutionists were not free of ethnocentricity. Western society of their time and its institutions formed the latest and thus the highest stage in the process of human evolution. As far as the family was concerned, most evolutionists held the position that the nuclear family of their time had evolved out of a family or household form that consisted of three generations. All this implied that evolutionists in the ongoing discussion of change in the European family took a positive position with regard to the disappearance of traditional family values that was inspired by the three-generation household, its familial solidarity, and its undivided family property.

Riehl and LePlay

A different view of the changing European family can be found in the work of Riehl and LePlay. Riehl (1823-1897) was a German theologist who also studied the history of art and culture. He can be seen as one of the first to engage in empirical family research, which he did during his journeys through Germany. Preparing for such a journey, he first studied the available statistical data about the area he planned to visit. Once in the area, he collected his own empirical material by interviewing the common people and "local experts" like family doctors, teachers, and ministers. His research results and his ideas on the family can be found in his book *Die Familie* ("The Family"), published in 1855.

Riehl concluded that the traditional three-generation household, *das ganze Haus*, was disappearing and was being replaced by two-generation household form, the nuclear family. The development of this nuclear family was for Riehl a threat to and a negation of the system of values he saw as typical for the traditional three-generation household. The values he referred to are familial solidarity, undivided familial property passing from generation to generation, paternal authority, and a strict, sex-based division of labor. Undivided familial property and its correlate, familial solidarity, were of such importance to Riehl because they provided old and sick family members with security. The disappearance of the traditional three-generation household had, according to Riehl, to be explained by the influence of liberalism and socialism on moral thinking. He strongly favored a moral reform that would stop and counter the influence of these new ideologies.[9]

In the same year that Riehl published his book, LePlay published a first edition of his study *Les ouvriers européens: études sur les travaux, la vie domestique et la condition morale des populations ouvrières de l'Europe* ("European workers: studies of the work, domestic life and moral condition of the working class in Europe"). Influenced by Comte, LePlay was convinced that the philosophical approach to social problems must give way to a scientific approach modeled after the methods of biology and the natural sciences. Through his work LePlay wanted to contribute to the restoration of social harmony in France, which he saw as having been destroyed by the French Revolution and its aftermath. Studying the family, according to LePlay, was the best way to study society. Changes in society are reflected in its families. According to LePlay, the condition of the family could best be judged by the analysis of its financial and time budgets, which reflected not only the economic situation of the family but also its moral and social condition.

LePlay used his journeys as a consulting mining engineer to study family life in different regions of Europe. To collect data about family life, LePlay carefully selected one family that could be considered typical for each particular area he visited. His data were the result of systematic participant observation during the one to four weeks he spent with the family he selected. In collecting his data on the family budget he used a questionnaire to record all financial, time, and productive actions of all household members. He reported his results in the form of a series of monographs, each having the same design. Apart from the family budget each monograph contained an explanation and interpretation of the budget and a discussion of the geographic and economic conditions in the region under consideration.

On the basis of his monographs, LePlay distinguished three family forms: *la famille patriarchale* ("the patriarchal family"), *la famille instabile* ("the unstable family"), and *la famille souche* ("the stem family"). His unstable family was the nuclear family of husband, wife, and unmarried children. The unstable family was in his opinion the result of individualism and industrialism. In this type of family, older children leave their parental home as soon as possible and no longer care for the well-being of their parents and other kin. Like Riehl, he was convinced that the unstable family was the main cause of the pauperism of the working class.

LePlay's stem family has the same characteristics as Riehl's traditional three-generation household. LePlay saw the stem family as the ideal family form, which should be the goal of the moral and social reforms he considered necessary. Common familial property and its correlate solidarity were for LePlay highly valued characteristics of the stem family. The authority of the head of the stem family was, according to LePlay, justified by the responsibility he had for the family property and the well-being of all individual family members. The presence of the stem family also had important implications for the larger society. In LePlay's opinion, this family produced citizens with high moral standards who valued hard work and respected social order and authority. Briefly, Le Play preferred citizens who matched the authoritarian type of state. The individualism, mobility, and differentiation of the unstable nuclear family produced a type of individual who did not fit into this authoritarian state.[10]

Marx and Engels

To complete the picture of diversity in nineteenth-century European family sociology, Marx and Engels must be discussed. Marx and Engels presented their ideas on the family in the context of their analysis of nineteenth-century society and its class antagonism. Their ideas on the family can be found in several sources: Engels' *Die Lage der arbeitenden Klassen in England* ("The position of the working classes in England") (1845), Marx's and Engels' "Communist Manifesto" (1848), and Engels' *Der Ursprung der Familie des Privateigentums und des Staats* ("The Origin of the Family, Private Property and the State") (1884). In their analysis of the antagonism between the bourgeoisie and the proletariat, Marx and Engels discussed the family life of both classes.

Their discussion of the bourgeois family pointed to the significance of monogamous marriage for the continuation of class differences and class antagonism. Monogamous marriage enabled the bourgeois husband to transfer his control over the means of production to his own children. To provide a husband with the certainty that the children of his wife were his own, monogamy was an important value for the wife in the bourgeois marriage. For the husband, however, this virtue was less important. The double standard, according to Marx and Engels, inherent in the bourgeois marriage, permitted the husband to have extramarital relations.

Mate selection in the bourgeois marriage was mainly based on considerations of power and control over the means of production. Because in the bourgeois family the husband exercised all power over the means of production, his wife and children were in a dependent position. By contrast, all housework and the socialization of and care for the children was the responsibility of the wife. This division of tasks and power between husband and wife was, according to Marx and Engels, the oldest form of antagonism and exploitation. For the sake of their own security, however, bourgeois women had to surrender themselves to such basic inequality and exploitation.

The family of the proletariat was in a different situation. Because of the low wages in the capitalistic system, husband, wife, and children had to have jobs. In this situation, an important basis for the difference in power between the husband and his wife and children disappeared. Because proletarians had no means of production to transfer, the basic reason for monogamy no longer existed. Although Marx and Engels were aware of the negative consequences of labor by the wife and children on family life, the nonexistence of economic dependency relationships had, in their opinion, to be evaluated in a positive way. The situation of the proletarian family opened a perspective on the development of new and more positive family relationships.

In the long run, when the means of production are collectively owned, Marx and Engels expected the liberation of women and the development of a new type of family. Collective possession of the means of production would imply that the monogamy of women would lose its social significance. Housework and the care of children would, they expected, be taken over by the collectivity. Both these factors would end the fundamental inequality between husbands and wives. Because the collectivity would be responsible for the care and socialisation of children, women would no longer have to be afraid for the consequences of a sexual relationship and would even have the possibility of terminating such relationships. About the type of family that would emerge as a result of the disappearance of the factors that shaped the bourgeois family, Marx and Engels had no concrete ideas. They only expected it to be quite different from the families they saw in their own time.[11]

Family and social integration

The three different visions of the changing nineteenth-century family discussed thus far are not isolated; they are consequences of and related to different concepts of society and societal order. The generally positive evaluation of the individualized nuclear family by most evolutionists must be seen in the perspective of their idea that in modern society social order is based on the contract principle. The critiques of Riehl and LePlay of the same nuclear family, and their positive evaluation of the three-generation household, were related to their idea that social order is a supra-individual phenomenon and that society needed the type of stable and rigid social order that existed prior to the French and the Industrial Revolutions. The vision of Marx and Engels of the family must be seen in their perspective that the existing class antagonism would lead to a situation wherein the present social order would be overthrown and replaced by a classless society, characterized by common ownership of the means of production. These three visions of social order represent the three main societal models that play a part in early European sociology.

Toennies

Toennies, in his book *Gemeinschaft und Gesellschaft* ("Community and Society"), brought these three different models to a synthesis. He reached this synthesis by giving each societal model its place in the course of history. Toennies' *Gemeinschaft* has all the characteristics of preindustrial and precapitalistic society. The social order in the *Gemeinschaft* is based on the same natural principles as in the three-generation household that Riehl calls *das ganze Haus* and that LePlay calls *la famille souche*. In Toennies' discussion the traditional three-generation household appears as the micro-model of the societal relationships in the *Gemeinschaft*. According to Toennies the *Gemeinschaft* was disappearing and being replaced by a type of society he called *Gesellschaft*. In the *Gesellschaft*, social order is based on the contract principle, for the *Gemeinschaft*-like relationships of the traditional three-generational household would hardly have any place in the *Gesellschaft* type of society, according to Toennies.

To the question whether or not the traditional three-generation family will persist, Toennies had little to say. Neither did he pay attention to the question of what type of family would fit into his *Gesellschaft*-like society. The neglect of these two questions by Toennies gets an extra dimension when we consider his opinion that a social order based on the contract principle could not be stable in the long run. Parties to such a contract are individuals who first, and above all, seek their own interests. Such contracts can only hide the antagonism in the interests of the individuals concerned. In the long run, he expects that the conflicting interests of the lower and higher classes in the *Gesellschaft* will result in the emergence of an international and socialist society.[12]

Durkheim

Without doubt social integration is the central theme in Durkheim's work, and his ideas on the family can best be discussed in this context. According to Durkheim, traditional or primitive societies were characterized by a low level of division of labor. All parts of such societies, to a large extent, are functionally equivalent. This implies that the segments of these societies have roughly similar and, in principle, conflicting interests. Therefore, the integration of societies with a poorly developed division of labor rests upon the presence of a "collective conscience" that exerts a strong influence on the individual's mind. The collective conscience of such societies gives rigid and detailed rules for individual behavior.

Modern societies were, by contrast, characterized by a highly developed division of labor. This results in much larger social differentiation and many more possibilities for individual differences. This increased division of labor and the accompanying differentiation lead to a change in the collective conscience. The impact of the collective conscience on the individual's mind and his thinking will be less extensive, and the rules for individual behavior will be less rigid and more general in character. The content of the collective conscience will also change. Individualistic values like the dignity of the individual, equality as a basis for human relationships, and equal opportunities for all individuals will come to play an important part.

Such a collective conscience can never be a sufficient basis for the integration of a society. Integration will mainly depend upon the interdependency derived from the division of labor. This interdependency is more than a purely economic market exchange of goods and services between individuals that only seek their own interests. Economic interdependency and the exchange of goods and services presuppose, according to Durkheim, the presence of a morality of cooperation. Durkheim compared the integration of societies having a highly developed division of labor with that of higher organisms and spoke in this context of "organic solidarity" (*solidarité organique*). The integration of societies with a poorly developed division of labor and thus a wide similarity between the composing parts reminded him of the integration of lower organisms. To this form of societal integration he gave the term "mechanical solidarity" (*solidarité méchanique*).

In some sectors of nineteenth-century society, according to Durkheim, mechanical solidarity still existed. In other sectors of society, especially industry, mechanical solidarity had disappeared. In these sectors a new division of labor existed, but the accompanying new collective morality still had to develop. Marx's economic crises and conflicting class interests were not, as Durkheim was aware, inevitable consequences of the new division of labor but followed from a lag in the development of a new, collective morality. In his publications and lectures, Durkheim appeared to be very interested in what the content of this new collective morality should be. In his opinion, the restorative political programs discussed in the work of Riehl and LePlay referred to the situation in those sectors of society where mechanical solidarity still existed. The rigid social order that restorative politicians propogated was not compatible with the increasing division of labor.

Liberal policies, on the other hand, referred to the present and according to Durkheim, temporary situation of industrial society. The liberal and rational concept of social order based on the common interest of individuals who first of all seek their own interests was, in his opinion, not a viable answer for the future. He saw individual needs as, in theory, unlimited. Without a collective moral authority to control the individual's needs and aspirations, the discrepancy between his needs and the means for their fulfillment will only increase. The answer of liberalism to the present situation in industry is purely economic and does not provide the moral authority necessary for the restriction of individual needs and aspirations.

On the Marxist vision of the situation in industrial society, Durkheim had in essence the same comment. The collective possession of the means of production was, in his opinion, an economic answer to a moral problem. The state and collective ownership stood too far from the individual to exert the moral power necessary for the restriction of individual needs. Durkheim suggested the formation of a guild-like system of professional corporations. Because these corporations stand closer to the individual, they can develop a moral code for each professional or economic sector of society. Problems of general interest should be solved through the interplay between the state and these professional corporations.[13]

During his stay in Bordeaux, Durkheim gave a series of lectures on the family, in which he presented a scheme for its historical development. Data on the history of the family law formed his empirical material. The final lecture of this series was published in 1921 by his pupil Mauss.[14] In this final lecture, Durkheim referred to this scheme when he formulated his "law of contraction" (*loi de contraction*). According to this law, the circle of kin members involved in familial life has decreased in size in the course of history. This decrease was accompanied by changing relationships between members of the familial group. One of these changes was a development in the direction of individual property. In explaining this development, Durkheim referred to the effect of the increasing social differentiation on individual differences. That such a development leads to the disappearance of common familial property must be explained by the fact that this institution persists only when the conscience of the group and its individual members are practically identical.

In recent history, according to Durkheim, the "conjugal family" (*famille conjugale*) developed out of the "paternal family" (*famille paternelle*). The paternal family, consisting of husband and wife and all their offspring, except daughters and their offspring, knows only collective property. For their existence, family members depend upon the common familial property. All this reminds us of LePlay's stem family and Riehl's traditional three-generation household. Durkheim's conjugal family reminds us of LePlay's "unstable family," for his conjugal family consists of husband, wife, and their unmarried offspring of minor age.

For his analysis of the conjugal family Durkheim used the Code Civil of 1892. Of the common familial property of earlier days, the Code Civil leaves only the common marital estate. Children can, after 1892, have their own property and under certain conditions even their own income. The only material bonds between parents and children are the duties of children to support their parents and the duty of parents to bequeath a fixed proportion of their estate to their children. All this brings the lifelong dependency of individuals on the common property of the paternal family to an end. The Code Civil also says that parental authority of the father lasts only until the age of majority or the marriage of the children. At the same time, the Code Civil offered the State, under certain conditions, the possibility to interfere even with this parental power. Finally, this law made an end to the possibility of breaching all ties between an individual and his family.

Commenting on the Code Civil, Durkheim dealt with the theme of familial solidarity. Familial solidarity could, according to Durkheim, be based on material and on personal motives. In the paternal family with its common property, solidarity is primarily based on material motives and secondarily on personal motives. In the conjugal family, with its individualized relationships, personal motives will be the main source and material motives the minor source of familial solidarity. Durkheim saw the parental obligation to bequeath their children a fixed proportion of their property as a survival of the common familial property of former days. In his opinion, this obligation did not fit with the individualized relationships and the person-oriented solidarity of the conjugal family. He also pointed to the negative impact of this obligation on social equality. Ties of heredity between parents and children mean that people are born rich or poor, which affects the division of labor in society. A division of labor based on such external factors does not agree with the individualistic morality of society. Only a division of labor based on internal factors, or differences in personal capacities and qualities, is in accordance with the individualistic content of the collective conscience of modern society. Consequently, Durkheim did not believe that such intergenerational ties of heredity could persist. As the French Revolution ended the possibility of transferring public functions from generation to generation, future legislation would made such a transfer of family property impossible. Durkheim was aware of the problems resulting from such a change. For the individual in his work, the well-being of his family and the future of his children were two important motivational forces. Making an end to the possibility for the man to bequeath the results of his work to his children would mean the disappearance of an important motivational force. In Durkheim's view the State would be too distant from the individual to serve as an alternative source of motivation. The marital relationship, Durkheim added, lacked a sufficient time-perspective for this purpose. In this respect, he saw a task for his guild-like professional corporations, which would be able to offer a man the possibility of identifying himself more with his work and less with his family.

In *Suicide* (*Le Suicide*, 1897) Durkheim again paid attention to the importance of marriage and the family for the individual—first by demonstrating a negative correlation between the occurrence of suicide and the integration of the individual into marital life and second by demonstrating a positive correlation between the frequency of suicide and divorce. In his interpretation of this correlation, he referred to the beneficial regulating influence of marriage on human, and especially male, passion. According to Durkheim the introduction of divorce, by itself, already weakened this influence and led to an anomic situation, which tended to increase divorces and suicides. Because the regulating influence of marriage is more important for men than women, the former are more affected. In Durkheim's view, because the needs of women are more conditioned by biological and organic factors, the regulating influence of marriage is less important for them. Because, in addition, monogamous marriage brings more restrictions on the freedom of women than of men, the introduction of divorce is an improvement of their situation and at the same time a protection against suicide.

A review of European family sociology during the nineteenth century

At the end of this description of nineteenth-century European family research some concluding remarks must be made:

1. Although several, if not many, nineteenth-century scholars deal with the family, family sociology had not emerged as a separate specialty at this period. There are no researchers calling themselves family sociologists, and even publications especially dealing with the family are an exception. Research and theoretical reflection on the family are in general embedded in activities aimed at other goals than the family itself. In sociology, the family is mostly discussed as one of the institutions to be studied in publications on the massive political and industrial changes in society at large. This even goes for LePlay, who studied the family largely because this institution reflected societal changes and conditions so well.

The second important context for nineteenth-century family research is the collection of empirical data on societal conditions for the sake of formulation of practical and political recommendations. In these activities poverty was the main problem, while the family budget and work by women and children were the most important topics studied in this context.

2. As far as sociology is concerned, many varied topics are discussed. These topics range from marriage and household forms to mate selection, inheritance, marital dissolution, marriage rituals, bride prices, rules for descent, and residential settlement. In this variety, some topics get special attention: household composition, familial solidarity, material relationships between family and kin, and paternal authority. The theoretical approach to these and other subjects is both historical and macrosociological. It is macrosociological not only because marriage and the family were studied as complexes of norms and values or as institutions but also because most nineteenth-century sociologists studied the family in its relationship to developments in other societal institutions or in society at large. That the evolutionists with their theories on the origin and the development of the family employed an historical perspective is quite obvious. The historical perspective is, however, also present in the work of most nineteenth-century sociologists who were primarily interested in the actual developments of their own time. Mostly these sociologists, to whom Rene Koenig refers as "present-day sociologists" (*Gegenwarts-soziologen*), used a more modest time dimension and analyzed actual problems in the perspective of changes during recent history.

A second important characteristic of nineteenth-century family sociology is its interest in the development of concepts and theories. Developing concepts and theories got far more attention than empirical research. LePlay with his family budgets, Riehl with his use of statistical data and fieldwork methods, and Durkheim with his quantitative analysis of the relationship between suicide and family membership are almost the only exceptions to this rule. In fact, most nineteenth-century sociologists derived their data from library research. The empirical evidence gathered in this way, however, more often functioned as illustration than as proof for the concepts and theories that were developed. Finally, it was characteristic of family sociology in this period that most scholars did not restrict themselves to a scientific analysis of marriage and the family but also engaged in moral evaluations and the development of political or practical recommendations.

3. This last remark brings us to the value-orientation of nineteenth-century family sociology. The three main political visions of this period have their representatives in family sociology. The vision of most evolutionists on social order and on the family correlates rather well with the basic ideas of liberalism. The ideas of Riehl and LePlay about the family in particular and about societal order in general reflected to a large extent the sentiments and ideas of the different political groups that aimed for a restoration of societal conditions prior to the French Revolution and the Industrial Revolution. Marx and Engels, finally, are the most extreme exponents of the socialistic visions that developed in nineteenth-century Europe.

The themes discussed in nineteenth-century family sociology can also be used to analyze its value-orientation. In analyzing recent changes in the family, most sociologists of the nineteenth century thought in terms of the disappearance of the traditional three-generation household and the emergence of a more individualistic type of nuclear family. In the analysis of both family types, most sociologists gave special attention to material relationships and to the way in which these relationships were connected to familial solidarity, paternal authority, and the position of the individual family member. This type of analysis was of special relevance for the situation in the old and new middle class of nineteenth-century European society. However, for the rapidly increasing mass of workers in the industrial centers, who lived under conditions of severe poverty, such an analysis was hardly relevant. Indeed, nineteenth-century sociologists gave little attention to the specific situation of the family life of these industrial workers. The important exception was the work of Marx and Engels. LePlay cannot be considered an exception because he defined the concept of worker so broadly that both the working class and farmers and tradesmen were included. Further, his conclusions were more relevant for families with a business of their own than for industrial workers. The main efforts during the nineteenth century to study the family of the industrial working class originated from outside sociology. The publications of individuals, private organizations, and government agencies on poverty were the main source of information and research on the working class family. Sociologists hardly appeared to be engaged in the collection or in the analysis of such information.

European and American parallels

To end this summary, some comparisons with American family research during the period 1860-1890 can be made. Following the arguments of the previous chapters, it must be concluded that, both in the United States and in Europe, family sociology had not yet emerged as a discipline or specialty with an identity of its own. As in Europe, family research in the United States is embedded in activities aimed at goals other than the family as such. Both in the United States and in Europe, early sociologists discussed marriage and the family in the context of macroscopic studies of social change. The second main context for family research was the broad and varied set of activities aimed at the relief of the consequences of urbanization and industrialization with their accompanying ideological and social changes. Reading Howard's discussion of the moral reformers (chapter I), the question arises whether or not the publications of most moral reformers can be considered as a contribution to family research or to family theory. Judged by the information Howard provides, neither the development of concepts and theories nor the presentation of empirical information played much of a part in the publications of most moral reformers. The presentation of a theological or philosophical evaluation seems to be the main purpose of their work.

Dike, the divorce reformer, and the Thwings, with their first American textbook on the family, were moral reformers who did not fit into this pattern. As founder of the New England Divorce Reform League, Samuel Warren Dike not only was a fierce opponent of divorce but also propagated the sociological study of and the collection of empirical data on the divorce problem. The Thwings started their textbook with a discussion of the history of the family that was based on the evolutionistic theories of their time and proceeded with a Christian dogmatic and prescriptive analysis of actual family problems. As appears from Howard's discussion of the period 1865-1890, initially the charity workers were inspired by the same set of ideas as the moral reformers. Soon, however, charity workers developed an empirical pragmatism that resembled the European attack on the poverty problem.

Considering research themes at a more general level, there is also some similarity between the United States and Europe. On both continents research themes were derived from the same process of social change. Under the influence of urbanization, industrialization, secularization, and individualization, the traditional rural family had lost its position as reference model and had given way to the modern, Western, nuclear family. Although at a general level, changes in the family on both continents have the same character, there was little overlap in the subjects American and European family scholars wrote about. Only the individualization of family relationships was common to both American and European family research. Other topics closely related to this theme differed. American researchers, as far as can be judged by Howard's discussion of the period 1865-1890, developed special interests in the position of women, in women's liberation, and above all in divorce. European family scholars tended to pay special attention to topics like household composition, material relationships in the kinship network, familial solidarity, and paternal authority.

The difference in interest can point to both differences in actual developments and to a difference in perception and appreciation of roughly the same changes. Further research on the history of the family on both continents will be needed to give a more accurate estimate in this respect. As far as differences in perception are concerned, research themes in American and European family sociology seem to indicate that American scholars were especially interested in the consequences of change in the family that affected the well-being of individual family members. European scholars, on the other hand, aimed at more general structural implications of changing family relationships for the provision of basic security to citizens in sickness and old age. We sense that the change from traditional to more modern family values took different forms, because individualization of family relationships in the United States seemed to lead to marital instability, while in Europe the same process of individualization seemed to disrupt parental authority and so affected intergenerational familial solidarity.

Although there is a difference in topical interest on the two continents, the theoretical orientation and the research methods were fairly similar. American sociologists developed, as did their European colleagues, a historical and macro-sociological perspective on the family. To a large extent this similarity in perspective can be explained by referring to the prominent influence of evolutionism in nineteenth-century sociology. As far as research methods are concerned, desk research and personal observations were the main sources of data for both American and European scholars. Although Howard is not explicit in this respect, other sources suggest that for American sociologists of this period empirical information, as in Europe, more often had an illustrative rather than a verification function.

Finally, it can be concluded that scientific and value-oriented reflection were integral parts of American research during this period. The early sociologists represented both the diehard version of liberalism (Sumner) and the more reform-oriented version of liberalism (Ward, Ross, and Giddings). The moral reformers represented a vision of society resembling European restorative political thinking. The type of family and society that moral reformers in the United States referred to had many characteristics in common with what Riehl and LePlay had in mind. Although the United States was the scene of several utopian experiments during this period, it is remarkable that family studies from a socialistic or Marxist point of view are missing from the record.

EUROPEAN (GERMAN) FAMILY RESEARCH 1900-1940

Introduction

In the preceding section of this chapter European family research till the end of the nineteenth century and American family research during the period 1865-1890 were compared. This section will be dedicated to development on both continents during the period 1900-1940.

Because of changes in sociology and cultural anthropology, which had a different national impact, the geographical basis of our comparison has to be adapted. During the nineteenth century, England, France, the United states, and Germany were most productive in sociology and family sociology. As a result of the dominant position of evolutionism and its profound influence on other nineteenth-century sociologists, sociology and cultural anthropology could hardly be differentiated. Sociology and cultural anthropology both seemed to be integral parts of one single discipline. Since the end of the nineteenth century and during the first two decades of the twentieth century, this situation has changed.

One of the main reasons for this change was the rising interest of cultural anthropologists in empirical field research. Boas in the United States and Malinowski and Radcliffe Brown in England all played leading parts in this new development.[15] This change led not only to a decline in the leading position of evolutionism but also to a differentiation in the object of study for cultural anthropology and sociology. As field research gained importance, cultural anthropologists set out to study nonwestern societies, while sociologists continued to concentrate their efforts on western society.

Because this book focuses on the history of research on western families, the activities of those sociologists and not of cultural anthropologists must be our main concern. Although during the period 1900-1940 the English concentrated on cultural anthropology, the United States, France, and Germany remained important centers of sociology. Judged by the number of studies, the United States and Germany were during this period the most productive in family sociology. Because in other European nations during this period the number of family studies was tiny, our intercontinental comparison can legitimately be restricted to the United States and Germany.

German Sociology

Compared to England and France, sociology in Germany developed relatively late. The first important contributions were made during the last two decades of the nineteenth century. Recognition of sociology as a separate academic discipline had to wait till the period between the First and the Second World Wars. During this period German sociology developed and prospered, but when the Nazis took over Germany in 1933, this growth came to a standstill for the next two decades. Looking over German sociology prior to 1933, two main streams can be distinguished: (1) the group of macro-sociologists primarily interested in the history and the future of Western civilization, (2) the group of analytical or formal sociologists, primarily interested in the form, and not in the content, of human interaction.

For the macro-sociologists the family only was one of the several institutions they discussed in their broad scope studies. To a large extent their work is a continuation of the European, nineteenth-century intellectual tradition. This not only goes for their research themes, but also for the research methods they employ. Primarily interested in the developments of concepts and theories, they used the library as their main source of data. Most of them willfully engaged in moral or political recommendations and evaluations. As far as marriage and the family are concerned, they add only a few to the ideas and perspectives developed during the nineteenth century. Further discussion of their work is for this reason unnecessary. For one group of macro-sociologists, the Frankfurter school, an exception must be made. Combining the ideas of Marx and Freud, the Frankfurter school developed an interesting vision on marriage and the family, first published after 1933, that will be discussed in one of the next sections.

The formal or analytical sociologists formed the second main stream in German sociology. Simmel, Vierkandt, and Von Wiese are representatives of this group. They all held the position that sociology should study social relationships by abstracting from their content and by focusing on their form. Following this strategy, they developed more or less elaborate systems for the classification and analysis of interpersonal relationships. In these classifications, the influence of Toennies' *Gemeinschaft* and *Gesellschaft* is visible.

These concepts offered more than a classification of societies. Both concepts aimed also at a classification of the interpersonal relations in both types of society. In their publications, Simmel, Vierkandt, and Von Wiese regularly paid attention to family relationships.[16] Because the development of concepts and classifications was their main concern, the systematic collection of empirical data played hardly any part in their work. Personal experiences and observations in daily life were their most important source of data. A full discussion of the contributions made by these three formal sociologists would go far beyond this context. Because Simmel's work influenced American sociology and Vierkandt was influential in German thinking about the family, only their contributions to family sociology will be discussed here.

Simmel

Simmel's most important sociological publications date from the last decade of the nineteenth century and the beginning of the twentieth century. His ideas on the forms of social interaction in the dyad and the triad are especially of interest for family sociologists. They can be found in his *Soziologie* ("Sociology") (1908). According to Simmel, it was characteristic for the dyad that its continuity depended entirely upon the participation of the two individuals concerned. The dyad missed the supra-individual character of the triad and larger groups. Such group developed a supra-individual "mental construction" (*Gebilde*) that continued to exist even when members left the group and were replaced by others. A second important feature of the dyad was its intimacy or its personal character. Although relations in the dyad were intimate, repetition of them inevitably led to commonness or triviality. The intimacy of the dyad also confronted its members with the problem of how to keep a proper balance of discretion. Knowing too little of each other or, as Simmel said, too much discretion created a distance between the partners in the dyad. Too little discretion created a situation wherein both partners no longer have something to offer each other. Both situations, knowing too little or too much of each other, endangered the continuity of the dyad.

In his further analysis of the dyad, Simmel pointed to additional consequences of the fact that there is no third party present. Some of the consequences are: Individuals in the dyad fully depend on each other; the individual cannot escape the responsibility for his actions; relationships in the dyad can neither be improved nor deteriorated; choices soon tend to have an all or nothing character; and finally, in the dyad there is no majority to outvote an individual. Marriage, however, according to Simmel, differs in some respects from the dyad in general. Because marriage is a social institution, the marital relation has a supra-individual aspect, a *Gebilde*, which the dyad misses. A second difference between marriage and the dyad has to do with the nature of the differences between the individuals involved. In the dyad these differences have a personal character. The basis for marriage, however, is the difference between the sexes, a general human characteristic.

According to Simmel, the presence of the third party was the essential structural difference between the dyad and the triad. Simmel saw the difference between the dyad and the triad as deeper than that between the triad and larger groups. In the triad individuals would never reach the same sense of unity as in the dyad. In the triad three different dyad-like relationships were possible. But each of these relationships would be influenced by the presence of the third party. Analysing the forms of social interaction in the triad, Simmel used the role of the third party as a starting point: Roles mentioned by Simmel are: mediator, referee, laughing third, and divide and rule. Analysing the triad, Simmel wrote particularly about the influence of the presence of a child on the relationship between the parents.

The relationship between the individual and the social institution is an important theme in Simmel's work. As stated before, for Simmel marriage differed from the dyad in general because it was a social institution. Marriage as an institution implied in his opinion a restriction in options for individual behavior. Reviewing recent developments in the marital institution, Simmel commented that because of the individualization of marriage, rules for individual behavior have become less strict and less detailed. Far from weakening the durability of marriage as an institution, this development significantly contributed to its continuity. Commenting on marriage, Simmel also elaborated the point that changes at the institutional and the individual level do not always go together. Either institutional or individual developments could lag behind.

As illustration of the latter, Simmel referred to the women's movement of his day. That so many women were looking for activities outside the home, a situation Simmel evaluated partially as positive and partially as negative, illustrated that the possibilities for the individual development of women lagged behind the institutional change that had transferred many economic activities from the home to the factory. To demonstrate the lagging behind of the institutional level, Simmel mentioned the dissatisfaction in many modern marriages, in his opinion the result of the discrepancy between the still traditional institutional rules for day-to-day married life, on the one hand, and the individual aspirations with regard to freedom, equality, and mutual understanding between spouses, on the other hand.

Being aware of tensions between marriage as an institution and individual wishes and aspirations, Simmel stressed the positive consequences of its institutionalization. Institutionalization, according to Simmel, led to a regulation and thus stabilization of marital behavior. Pressure from law and existing social norms led to the continuity of marriages that otherwise would have been dissolved. He was aware of this effect both for marriages that morally would be better dissolved and for other marriages that would have been dissolved for only incidental or temporary reasons. Notwithstanding the former, Simmel valued the institutional influences against marital dissolution more postively than negatively. His arguments for this evaluation were that this institutional pressure provided individuals with stability and consistency in their lives.

The family was for Simmel an intermediate structure (*Zwischengebilde*) between the individual and society. For each individual, the family was both a multifaceted complex of separate individuals and, in relation to society, a closed unit. In recent history, according to Simmel, the size of the family fell when the nuclear family replaced the traditional three-generation household. A second recent change Simmel points to is that the family lost its importance as an organization that performed many different functions. As a consequence, relations in the family have become more person-oriented and less task-oriented. Changing functions of the family also changed the basis of its integration. The integration of the family no longer rested on the variety of interests associated with the different functions that the family used to have, but on personal and biological ties. Placing these changes in the family in a larger context, Simmel pointed to the differentiation of society, which had led to a specialization in task-oriented and person-oriented relationships. Both types of relationships required, in Simmel's opinion, their own form of institutions. The nuclear family with its small size and, because of that, its potentiality for intimate and personal relations, fitted, as Simmel saw it, very well into an individualized and differentiated society where there was a separation of task-oriented and person-oriented forms of social interaction.[17]

Vierkandt

Vierkandt, the second German formal sociologist to be discussed, published mainly in the 1920s and 1930s. His major work, *Gesellschaftlehre* ("Study of Society") was dedicated to the classification of interpersonal relations and to the analysis of the basic principles for the integration of the human group. In the last section of his *Gesellschaftslehre* (first published in 1928), Vierkandt applied his ideas on social relations and social integration to the analysis of a number of important groups in society. One of these groups was the family. Analyzing the family, Vierkandt combined his formal sociological approach with a historical and macro-sociological perspective. In fact, he started his discussion of the family with a historical and macro-sociological analysis. Dealing with the recent history of the family, he referred to developments like the replacement of the traditional three-generation household by the nuclear family; the declining importance of kinship ties; the disappearance of familial solidarity; increasing independence or selfishness of grown-up children towards their parents; a decay of parental authority; a decreasing number of family functions; the increasing personal significance and the decreasing material significance of family relationships for the individual; the individualization of family relationships in general; and the emergence of the romantic marriage in particular.

Declining familial solidarity and the emergence of romantic marriage were two developments Vierkandt seriously deplored. As he saw it, romantic marriage was based on the idea that marriage aimed primarily at the satisfaction of the erotic or sensual-psychic passion of both partners. For Vierkandt this implied that the quality and durability of marriage fully depended upon the quality and the continuity of this passion. Vierkandt could not agree with this purely individualistic vision of marital integration. In his opinion, the wedding itself started a process leading to a form of integration independent from the personal needs and wishes of both partners. The part erotic passion played in this supra-individual integration could vary considerably. For this reason he introduced the concepts "situation-oriented marriage" (*Situationehe*) and "inner-oriented marriage" (*Neigungsehe*). His comment on both concepts is very brief. Integration in the situation-oriented marriage was mainly based on forces working from the outside environment (e.g., material interests, social control of neighbors and kin). In the inner-oriented marriage integrative forces mainly worked from the inside; personal love and affection were their most important basis.

Both the development of the romantic marriage and the decline of intergenerational solidarity were in Vierkandt's view results of the individualization of family relationships. That he was concerned about these developments must be seen in the perspective of his ideas on social integration. In his theory, individualization of the relationships in marriage and the family threatened the *Gemeinschaft*-like character of these institutions. *Gemeinschaft*-like relationships were, according to Vierkandt, most important for the continuity of society. In these relationships the individual learned the basic skills required for the participation in stable *Gesellschaft*-like relationships. Considering the increasing predominance of *Gesellschaft*-like relationships in society, Vierkandt, worried about who, when the family also lost its *Gemeinschaft*-like character, would be able to teach youth the basic skills required for successful participation in stable *Gesellschaft*-like relationships.[18]

Frankfurter School

From its foundation in 1923, the *Frankfurter Institut fuer Sozialforschung* was dedicated to the study of sociohistorical problems. With the appointment in 1930 of Horkheimer as its director, the

Institute also set out to do empirical research. The central theme of the research project that Horkheimer and his associates at the Institute developed can be put in a simple phrase: "family and authority." Working on this project, economic, philosophical, historical, anthropological, sociological, and psychological contributions were made. Empirical studies carried out in this project dealt with moral standards for sexual behavior, authoritarian attitudes among both workers and employers, attitudes of youth with regard to familial authority, and cross-national differences in opinions on familial authority. In 1933, takeover by the Nazis brought a sudden end to the activities of the Institute; Horkheimer and most of his associates went abroad. In 1936 a volume containing the various contributions to the project was published by Horkheimer in Paris, as "Studies of Authority and the Family" (*Studien ueber Autoritaet und Familie*). Horkheimer's introduction to this very influential publication gives the theoretical frame of reference of the project. The following discussion of Horkheimer's ideas is based on this introductory chapter.[19]

In Horkheimer's view, history could be seen as a sequence of periods, each characterised by the emergence, the establishment, and the decline of a type of social order that could be explained by the mode of production existing in the period considered. During a certain interval in such a period, there existed a harmony between the mode of production, the social relations of production, the class relationships, and the ideological superstructure of society. Each mode of production produced not only its own social inequalities but also the type of personality that had learned to accept these inequalities. The acceptance of such inequalities by the individual was termed by Horkheimer "authority." He coined this use of the term. Horkheimer's view of history implied that each period was characterized by a different type of authority. Apart from the state, the educational system, and other societal institutions, the family played an important part in producing a certain type of authority. Against authority in accordance with the existing mode of production Horkheimer had no objections. Such a type of authority was in the interest of all concerned. But, as Horkheimer said, authority once in existence had a tendency to live a life of its own and to maintain itself. As soon as new modes of production emerged, this, once legitimate authority would develop into a barrier to the further development of society and the individual. According to Horkheimer, such a situation existed in the western world of the 1920s and the 1930s. The existing social inequality and authority in those days no longer were in the interest of the individuals concerned. Dealing with the family, he pointed to the part played by the patriarchal bourgeois conjugal family since the end of the nineteenth century in the maintenance of a type of authority that had outlived itself. The power of the father in this type of family was, in Horkheim's view, based on his role as a provider. The financial power resulting from this role enabled the father to satisfy or to neglect the wishes of his wife and children. The price the man paid for this position was that, being responsible for the well-being of his wife and children, he was forced to accept the existing authority in the world outside the family. In doing this, he was actively encouraged by his wife.

From their early youth on, children in the patriarchal bourgeois family became accustomed to authoritarian power relationships. In addition, they learned at an early age that the acceptance of authority brings advantages that could hardly be obtained otherwise. The suppression of sexuality and eroticism in the patriarchal bourgeois family, according to Horkheimer, had negative consequences for the development of the personality of the children. By suppressing sexuality and eroticism, this type of family bound the energy that otherwise could have been used for the development of creativity and a questioning attitude towards authority. At the end of his analysis Horkheimer concluded that in the 1930s the first signs of the decline of the patriarchal bourgeois family were already visible.

Horkheimer and his associates were not the only scholars during the 1920s and 1930s taking a left-wing political position in the analysis of marriage and the family. Theodor Geiger, inspired by socialism as he was, developed an interest in social inequality. Using official statistical data as empirical material, he published on intergenerational mobility and illegitimacy. In his study of illegitimacy, he investigated to what extent the nearly identical legal rights of legitimate and illegitimate children were reflected in the social positions reached by these two categories of children.[20]

Social workers and psychologists

To complete this brief overview of German family research, one more category of studies must be mentioned. At several places in Germany during the 1920s and 1930s the needs of social work and welfare policy generated family research, some of which is clearly sociological. One of the important centers in this respect was the German Academy of Social and Educational Work for Women (*"Deutsche Akademie fuer soziale und pedagogische Frauenarbeit"*). In a rather short period (1930-1933) Alice Salomon and her assistants at this institute published a large number of family studies. The series of reports of this institute run to twelve volumes. One of the best-known studies of this series dealt with the problem of whether or not the family was still a stable and well integrated unit.[21]

The empirical material for this study consisted of 182 case studies that were inspired by LePlay's research methods. The data in these case studies were the result of participant observation, interviews, and the collection of data registered in the records of official agencies. Although inspired by the research methods of LePlay, the project did not aim at the collection of data on the family budget. Husband-wife relationships, socialization of children, and relationships between family and kin were the main topics of investigation.

In the same period, psychologists and educators, confronted with problems stemming from the world of social work, engaged in family research. Directed by William Stern and Martha Mushov, the Psychological Institute in Hamburg did research on the effect of the presence of a stepmother on children, and on the problems met by unwed mothers in the socialization of their children.[22] The educator Adolf Buseman researched the relationship between birth order and school achievement.[23] Austria was also a center for psychologists studying family and child development. Karl and Charlotte Buehler at the Vienna Psychological Institute directed research on the effect of social class on the personality development of children. At the same institute, researchers used participant observation as a method for the study of interaction processes between parents and children.[24] Finally, the Vienna Psychological Institute was also the center from which Jahoda, Zeisel and Lazars-

feld did their interesting and much quoted study of the effect of
unemployment on the daily life and family relationships in the town
of Mariental.[25]

AMERICAN AND GERMAN FAMILY RESEARCH 1900-1940

As can be seen in the preceding pages, most German contributions
to family sociology during the years 1900-1940 date from the period
between the two World Wars. On the American scene, for the time
span 1865-1940, the years 1890-1920 can be characterised as a
transitional period between early American family research and
the important formative decades between both World Wars. Consequently, in comparison of American and German family sociology, a focus on the 1920s and 1930s will be most relevant. As in the
comparison for the nineteenth century, we will successively deal
with the position of family research as a discipline, major research
themes, theoretical frameworks, research methods, and value
orientations.

Chapter III contains most of the information necessary to estimate the position of family sociology as a discipline with an identity
of its own. Reviewing the situation during the 1920s and 1930s, it
can be concluded that American family sociology came close to its
establishment as a full-fledged specialty. There are several arguments justifying such a conclusion: (1) Studies dealing directly and
specifically with the family were published on a regular basis; (2)
the number of scholars dedicating a large proportion of their time
to family research increased; (3) there developed an organizational
structure contributing significantly to the emergence of family
sociology as a discipline, and (4) the field in which family scholars
were active expanded considerably.

The development of an organizational structure for the emergence
of family sociology began with the Family Section of the American
Sociological Association in 1924. In 1928 a section in *Social Forces*
where articles about the family could be published began under
Ernest R. Groves as editor. Groves also began in 1934 the annual
gathering of theorists and practitioners interested in the family as
the Groves Conference on Marriage and the Family. Finally, a
special organization, the National Council on Family Relations,

began in 1938. Providing a structure wherein both researchers and those working directly with family problems participated, the NCFR established its own journal. In the establishment of this journal, *Marriage and Family Living*, Ernest Burgess played a leading part. Renamed in 1964 the *Journal of Marriage and the Family*, this journal continues to be the most influential source of research theories, methods, and reports on the family.

As we have seen in chapters II and III, social work used to be an important field of activity for family scholars. During the 1920s and 1930s two new important fields developed. Courses in the preparation for marriage and parenthood begun by Ernest Groves in 1924 at Boston University soon spread acrosss the United States giving new employment opportunities to family specialists. Second, a new branch of social work emerged, as marriage counselors found an increasing demand for their services by couples already married. The Association of Marriage Counselors was founded in 1940.

The developments discussed thus far all indicate a growth and expansion of the family field. As important as this growth itself is the emergence of an influential set of research problems and theoretical concepts all aiming at the study of the family as a small group. Initiated by sociologists and social psychologists before 1920, the interactional approach became an important framework for the study of the family. Ernest Burgess, with his influential article in 1926, and Willard Waller, with his elaboration of the interactional framework in his book *The Family*, contributed significantly to this development.[26] Ernest Groves also helped to focus attention on the family as a small group. He did this both in his capacity as successful innovator of courses for marriage and parenthood and in his position as trainer of marriage counselors. Most helpful in the diffusion of the set of concepts and research problems centered on the family as a small group was the fact that both Burgess and Groves held influential and strategic positions the academic world and the organizational field of family sociology.

Notwithstanding all these developments, family sociology still had not reached its establishment as a full-fledged specialty. Family sociology used concepts and methods drawn from such fields as social psychology, social work, therapy and education, but those who were interested in and working with these ideas and these data continued to think of themselves as sociologists, or educators, or social workers. It took some time after 1940 before the concept of family sociology as a full-time specialty to which a scholar could devote a whole career became accepted. Kingsley Davis claims to have used the term "family sociology" first; the first academic title of family sociologist is claimed by Justin Landis and the University of California at Berkeley. Equally early was the appointment of Reuben Hill at Iowa State College in 1944 to a post clearly calling for teaching, graduate training, and research only in marriage and the family. Centers devoted full time to research on the family followed after 1950.

Compared to the American scene, the development of the field of family research had progressed less far in Germany. From all the publications dealing with the family, a smaller proportion than in the United States concentrated on the family directly. The formation of a nucleus of scholars especially interested in the family was still in its first and preliminary stage during the period prior to World War II. Promising initiatives in this direction could be seen at the *Frankfurter Institut fuer Sozialforschung*, where Horkheimer and his associates worked on the theme family and authority, and the *Deutsche Akademie fuer soziale und pedagogische Frauenarbeit*, where Alice Salomon directed a research team especially interested in the problems related to social work and welfare policy; and, finally, among psychologists and educators there was developing an interest in processes inside the family. Supporting structures like an organization of family scholars and the publication of journals especially dedicated to the family were missing.

Family studies published during this period mainly aimed at a contribution to the public discussion on the political and moral consequences of changing family norms and values. Publications contributing to more specific applied fields such as welfare policy, social work, and clinical psychology played a minor part. As far as theoretical concepts and ideas were concerned, no dominating approach nor any clearly visible and well organized theoretical school was present. The field of family research, far less developed than in the United States, contained, however, some promising starting points for further growth and development. These promising developments came to an abrupt end when the Nazis came to power in 1933. As a consequence of the changed political climate, most sociologists either went abroad or moved to other jobs and functions. As far as research topics were concerned, German family scholars during most of the period 1900-1940 continued to be interested in themes that had played an important part in nineteenth century European family research. Such topics as the transition from the three-generation household to the nuclear family, changing relationships in the family, declining familial solidarity, and weakening paternal authority still received considerable attention. In addition to these, some new themes came to the fore: marital integration and stability, the position of women, socialization and personality development, and, finally, social work problems. At a general level some of these were similiar to those in American family research of the 1920s and the 1930s. In defining problems related to these themes, German scholars, in comparison to their American colleagues, showed a special interest in changing norms and values and in the consequences of these changes in society at large for family structure. Interactional aspects, involving studies of the internal operating of families and consequences for the individuals concerned, received much less attention than in American studies dealing with the same themes.

This difference is also reflected in the theoretical orientation of family sociology in the two countries. The theoretical orientation of German family research during this period was deeply influenced by the historical and macro-sociological intellectual tradition of nineteenth-century European sociology. This held even for the innovative formal sociologists Simmel and Vierkandt. These formal sociologists were primarily interested in the social forms of small social groups, not in the content of social interaction, but their analysis of relations and processes within the family was embedded in the macro-sociological discussion. Another mixture of macro- and micro-sociological perspectives could be found in the work of Horkheimer and his associates, which was based on a combination of concepts from Marx and Freud. A more specific interest for the family as a small group could be found among some German psychologists and educators who developed ideas and concepts resembling the American interactional approach, William Stern

and Martha Muchov, and Karl and Charlotte Buehler. The developing German interest in the family as a small group led to some
similarity to the American situation, where the interactional perspective was dominant. The profound influence of the historical
and macro-sociological approach in Germany outweighed the
significance of this similarity.

At the level of research methods there was a difference between
the United States and Germany. In American family research
during the 1920s and the 1930s the fieldwork collection of new
empirical data had developed into an essential and basic require-
ment. Although there was a developing interest in the collection of
empirical data in Germany, library research and personal observations were the main sources of data. This difference in research
methods was not a pure matter of sophistication, but also had to
do with dominating research problems. As can be seen in the previous discussion, historical changes in family norms and values
formed an important research topic. For this type of problem, the
collection of empirical data at the present time could only be of
limited value and could only be one of the sources of the wide
variety of empirical evidence needed. More or less the same kind of
comment is possible in relation to the activities of the formal sociologists Simmel and Vierkandt. Personal experiences and the analysis
of existing literature were a sufficient basis for the first steps in
developing a system of concepts with regard to the forms of social
interaction.

The development of American family sociology into a science,
for which the collection of empirical evidence directly from families
formed an essential condition, was accompanied by the growing
conviction that sociology should refrain from moral evaluations
and political recommendations. Although this idea was also developing in Germany, as can be seen from the activities of Alice Salomon
and her research team, most family scholars discussed here continued
to combine a scientific and evaluating approach to their subject.
Of these scholars, Horkheimer and Vierkandt differed most in
opinions and value orientations. To Vierkandt, the individualization
of husband-wife and parent-child relationships was a matter of
serious concern because of its threatening implications for a stable
societal order. Horkheimer and his associates, however, had a

positive view of the same process of individualization. Their negative appreciation of the existing social order led to a severe critique of authoritarian family relationships and a positive view of egalitarian and more democratic marital and family relationships.

Because of the changing concepts of the role of the sociologist, explicit moral or political evaluations of existing family relationships were rather hard to find in American family studies dating from the 1920s and 1930s. The most notable exceptions in this respect were Carl C. Zimmerman and Pitirim Sorokin. Both of these scholars tended to prefer the traditional rural family above the modern individualized family in America's urban centers. For most other scholars active during this period, their choice of research topics rather than their explicit statements must be used as an indicator of their value orientations.

The rather general tendency during this period to study the family as a small group and the sharp decline in interest in its institutional aspects is very informative in this respect. These two narrowly related developments indicate, first, that family scholars no longer saw much relevance in reacting to a public discussion on the *pro* and *contra* of changing family norms and values of the developing modern nuclear family with its individualized relationships. This conclusion is further supported by the kind of concepts used in the interactional approach to family study. The concept of marriage and the family as an interaction process, the idea of marital adjustment between individuals with different expectations, the defining of family crises and divorce in terms of a differentiation in individual role expectations and definitions, the special interest in the relationship between family processes and the personality of the individuals concerned—all these ideas and concepts match very well with and have the potentiality to contribute to the solution of problems related to individualizing family relationships.

The very low attention to the interrelationships between the family and other societal institutions, and the special interest in education and counseling in family matters, indicate that information and assistance at the level of the individual and his family, not structural or moral reforms, were seen as the basic strategy for dealing with changing family relationships. Beside the nature of central concepts and research themes in the interactional approach, there were other indicators of the orientation of the main stream of American family sociology in support of the realization of modern, individualized family values. One of these indicators was the engagement of several scholars in the field of marriage education and counseling. Another was that many scholars not only saw their research as a contribution to the body of scientific knowledge as such but also pointed to its relevance for counseling and education. That American family sociology reacted successfully to the social developments around marriage and the family can be seen not only from the success of marriage classes at many colleges, and the rapid development of marriage counseling, but also from the increasing public demand for information and advice regarding marriage and parenthood.

Comparing the American and the German situations, some interesting conclusions can be put forward. The first is that German family sociology showed a larger variety in moral and political evaluations of changing family norms and values. In American family sociology, by contrast, except for the minority represented by Zimmerman and Sorokin, the situation is close to a consensus in favor of the study of ongoing and developing modern family relationships. Second is that individualizing family relationships in Germany and the United States led to reactions at a different level. German family scholars appear to have a special interest in the moral or political implications of changing family norms and see these implications in the perspective of the situation in society at large. However different the views of Horkheimer and Vierkandt may be, there is a striking similarity in their concern with these types of consequences. In the United States, the emergence of modern and individualized family values led family scholars to a special concern with processes and relations at the level of the individual family.

DISCUSSION

The comparison in this chapter of trends in American and European family research has revealed both parallels and differences. In the commentary on this, differences have up to now had most attention. Starting this discussion with a summary of the main parallels will to some extent make up for this bias. Reviewing events in the United States and Europe since the nineteenth century, it can be concluded that family research on both continents, generally speaking, developed according to the same pattern:

1. On both continents, family research started out as a partial activity of sociologists and particularly of those interested in social or moral reform. When during the twentieth century the number of studies especially devoted to the family increased, family research developed into an activity in its own right.

2. At the outset both American and European scholars were primarily interested in the study of changing family norms and values. In the course of the twentieth century, scholars on both continents developed an interest in the inner workings of the family, a development that led to theoretical diversity. In addition to the macro-sociological, and often historical, approach there developed an interest in the use of social-psychological and psychological concepts and ideas in family analysis.

3. In the domain of research methods, both continents were the scene of a shift from studies based on library research and personal impressions to studies relying on empirical data collected through field work. Gradually, the idea developed that empirical research is an essential condition for family study. With the growing acceptance of this idea, the norm developed that family scholars should refrain from moral and political evaluations. Their share in the solution of family problems should be restricted to the production of empirically verified knowledge. It is significant that the development of this norm more or less coincided in time with the growing importance of applied family research.

Though, on close inspection, these trends can be seen at work on both continents, it is quite obvious that in the United States development along these lines had progressed much further. Differences discussed in the previous section suggest, that the nineteenth-century intellectual tradition of family research continued to be influential in Europe of the 1920s and 1930s, while there was a sharp decline in this respect in the United States.

Being aware of the rather meager geographical basis for our comparison of American and European trends during the first four decades of the twentieth century, it is the more interesting that the main results of this comparison also apply to the first decades after World War II. By then family research in Europe had a much wider geographical basis. As appears from the two international trend reports of Hill (1945-1956) and Mogey (1957-1968), scholars in most western European nations were actively engaged in family research by the beginning of the 1950s, while several nations in northern Europe followed somewhat later. Most of the data Hill and Mogey present in their trend reports differentiate only between the United States on the one hand and the rest of the world on the other. As far as they provide us with more specific regional information, it can be concluded that during the period 1945-1968 there was, both in the United States and in Europe, a trend towards greater public and academic acceptance of family sociology as a specialty in its own right. Further, scholars on both continents showed an increasing interest in the collection of empirical data and the use of modern methods for their analysis. Existing differences in research methods gradually diminished, with the United States in the position of trend setter. More deep-seated differences during this period were visible in the domain of research problems and theoretical orientation. Throughout the whole period European scholars had a relatively strong interest in macroscopic family studies and in the analysis of transactions between the family and other social institutions, while their theoretical orientation was more macro-sociological. By contrast, their American colleagues more frequently applied interactional concepts, while their publications more frequently dealt with topics specific for the study of the family as a small group.

To explain these, in the long run rather consistent, transoceanic differences in theoretical orientation and in interest in research topics, two hypotheses will be formulated. To test these hypotheses, more research on the history of both the family and family research will be needed. One possible explanation for the differences discussed here is that traditional family norms and values had deeper historical roots in Europe than in the United States, so that their replacement by modern ones in Europe not only took place more gradually but also led to different family problems. The relatively broad interest of European scholars in familial solidarity and related topics, on the one hand, and the early interest American scholars developed in divorce and the position of women, on the other hand, to some extent support this hypothesis. The second hypothesis has to do with the reaction of public opinion and the political system to family problems met by a large and increasing number of people. In Europe, there was and still is a tendency to stress the general social aspects of such problems. In solving them, public opinion and the political system more often tend to rely on actions on the part of government or other major social institutions. In the family or welfare policy of most European nations, general measures for the benefit of the total population or for other large sections of the population are more frequent than in the United States. The child allowance systems and the health or health-insurance programs in most European nations are examples of such general measures. In the United States there has been and still is a stronger tendency to stress the individual aspects of family problems. Strategies for their solution more often tend to follow the model of providing to the individual through education, advice, counseling, or information the means to solve his own problems. In social or welfare policy, programs aiming at specific groups with very special problems are more frequent. These differences in the workings of public opinion and the political system tend to generate different contributions from the social sciences. Stressing the general social aspects of family problems will stimulate the interest of family scholars in macro-sociological theories and research problems. The tendency to stress the individual aspects of family problems and to think in terms of the self-reliant individual, who may need help or advice, will stimulate the interest in micro-sociological theories and research topics. This type of theory and research is most likely to produce results that individuals can apply at the level of their own life and families.

NOTES

1. Reuben Hill, "Sociology of Marriage and Family Behaviour 1945-56: A Trend Report and Bibliography," *Current Sociology* 7 (1958): 1-98; John Mogey, "Sociology of Marriage and Family Behavior 1957-68: A Trend Report and Bibliography," *Current Sociology* 17 nos. 1-3 (1969): 1-364.

2. The comparison of developments in American and European family research during the period 1865-1940 is based both on Howard's dissertation and on my own dissertation. Louis Th. van Leeuwen, "Marriage and the Family as a Subject of Sociological Study: A Historical Overview of the History of a Sub-discipline, Especially with Regard to the Situation in the Netherlands," *Het gezin als sociologisch studie-object: een historisch overzicht van de ontwikkeling van een sub-discipline, speciaal net het oog op de situate in Nederland.* Wageningen, the Netherlands Landbouwhogeschool, Afdeling Sociologie Westers: 1976.

3. Charles Booth, *Life and Labour of the People in London*, 17 vols. (London: Macmillan, 1889-1891); B. Seebohm Rowntree, *Poverty: A Study of Town Life* (London: Macmillan, 1906).

4. Ernst Engel, "The Production and Consumption Relationships in the Kingdom of Sachsen," *"Die Productions und Consumtionsverhaeltnisse des Koenigreichs Saechsischen."* Zeitschrift des Statistischen Bureaus des Koeniglich Saechsischen Ministeriums des Innern, vol. 3, 1857, reprinted 1895.

5. For a discussion of the activities of Alexander Von Oettingen the reader is referred to Schwaegler's interesting study on the origin and history of family sociology, especially that of Germany. G. Schwaegler, "Family Sociology: Origins and Development," *Soziologie der Familie: Ursprung und Entwicklung*, (Tuebingen: Mohr, 1975).

6. A. Oberschall, *Empirical Social Research in Germany, 1848-1914*, (Paris/The Hague: Mouton, 1965; New York: Humanities, 1965).

7. C.B.S., "History of the Collection and Publication of Official Statistical Data in the Netherlands" *(Geschiedenis van de statistiek in het Koninkrijk der Nederlanden)* (The Hague: Central Statistical Office of the Dutch Government, 1902); H. Rijken van Olst, "Introduction to Statistics, vol. 1 *(Inleiding tot de statistiek, deel 1)* (Assen, The Netherlands: Van Gorcum & Co., 1966).

8. Most helpful in making this selection were G. Schwaegler, "Family Sociology"; Rene Koenig, "Family Sociology" *(Soziologie der Familie)* in *Handbuch der Empirischen Sozialforschung* (Stuttgart: Enke, 3 vols. 1967-1969) pp. 172-305.

9. G. Schwaegler, "Family Sociology."

10. This discussion of LePlay's work is based on G. Schwaegler. See also C. D. Saal, "The Farmer's Family in the Netherlands" *(Het Boerengezin in Nederland)* (Assen, Netherlands: Van Gorcum & Co., 1958); N. S. Timasheff, *Sociological Theory: Its Nature and Growth* (New York: Random House, 1967); P. G. Frédéric LePlay, *Les ouvriers européens. Etudes sur les travaux, la vie domestique, et la condition morale des populations*

ouvrières de l'Europe. (Paris: Imprimerie impériale, 1855; 2 ed. Tours: A. Mame et fils, 6 vols. 1877-1879)

11. This discussion of the vision of Karl Marx and Friedrich Engels on the family is mainly based on their *Communist Manifesto* (New York: Washington Square Press, 1964), first published in German in 1848, and on Engels' "The Origin of the Family, Private Property, and the State" (New York: International Publishers, 1942), first published in 1884 as *Der Ursprung der Familie, des Privateigentums und des Staats.* To remain brief, no attention is paid to the interesting way in which Engels incorporates Morgan's ideas on the origin of the family in his book.

12. F. Toennies, *Gemeinschaft und Gesellschaft; Grundbegriffe der reinen Soziologie* (Leipzig: Fues's Verlag, 1887; 2ed. Berlin: K. Curtius, 1912); Eng. trans. by Charles P. Loomis (Cincinnati: American Book Co., 1940).

13. This general discussion of Durkheim is based on Anthony Giddens, *Capitalism and Modern Social Theory: An Analysis of Marx, Durkheim and Max Weber* (Cambridge, England: University Press, 1971); A Discussion of his series of lectures on the family can be found in G. Simpson, "A Durkheim fragment," *A.J.S.* 70, no. 5 (1965): 527-36.

14. Emile Durkheim and Marcel Mauss, "The Conjugal Family" ("La famille conjugale"), *Revue Philosophique* XCI (January-June, 1901): 1-14. A translation of this article is published by G. Simpson.

15. For a discussion of the increasing interest of cultural anthropologists for field work see M. Harris, *The Rise of Anthropological Theory* (London: Crowell, 1968). Boas' first ethnological expedition to the Kwakiutl Indians was in 1886; Radcliffe Brown's first field expedition was to the Andaman Islands in 1906-08; Malinowski went for field work to Australian New Guinea and the Trobriand Islands in 1914-18.

16. For the contributions of Simmel and Vierkandt we refer to footnotes 17 and 18. Leopold Von Wiese (Leopold Max Walter von Wiese und Kaisenwaldau), *Allgemeine Soziologie als Lehre von den Beziehungen und Beziehungsgebilden der Menschen,* 2 vols. (Muenchen und Leipzig: Duncker & Humblot, 1924-29).

17. This discussion of Simmel's ideas on the family is based on A. Bevers, "Marriage and the Family in the Sociology of Georg Simmel" (*Huwelijk en gezin in de sociologie van Georg Simmel Sociale Wetenschappen* 18, no. 3 (1974): 189-213.

18. This discussion of Vierkandt is based on A. Vierkandt, A Brief Study of Society (*Kleine Gesellschafts lehre*) (Stuttgart: F. Enke, 2ed 1928; 1936, reprint, 1949); trans. 1975 (New York: Arno Press).

19. This discussion of the ideas of the Frankfurter School is mainly

based on a Dutch translation of Horkheimer's introductory essay in "Studies of Authority and Family" (*Studien ueber Autoritaet und Familie*). M. Horkheimer "Authority and family" (*Autoriteit en gezin*) (Den Haag, Netherlands: Stichting Uitgeverij, N.V.S.H., 1970).

20. Theodor Geiger, "A Statistical study of those born out of wedlock" (*Zur Statistik der Unehelichen*), *Allgemeines Statistischen Archiv* (1918-19) 212-20; *Das uneheliche Kind und seine Mutter im Recht des neuen Staates: Ein Versuch auf des Basis kritischer Rechtsvergleichung* (Munich: Schweitzer, 1920); *Die soziale Schichtung des deutschen Volkes: Soziographischer Versuch auf statistischer Grundlage* (Stuttgart: Enke, 1932).

21. Alice Salomon and Marie Baum, eds., *Present-day family life*. Das Familienleben in der Gegenwart: 182 Familienmonographien herausgegeben von Alice Salomon und Marie Baum, unter mitarbeit von Annemarie Niemeyer und anderen (Berlin: F.A. Herbig Verlagsbuchhandlung, G.M.B.H. 1930) (Deutsche Akad. fuer soziale und paedagogische Frauenarbeit, Berlin. Forschungen ueber "Bestand und Erschuetterung der Familie in der Gegenwart, Bd. 1).

22. William Stern, "Introduction" (*Einleitung*) in Hanna Kuehn, "Psychological Research on the Stepmother Problem" (*Psychologischen Untersuchungen ueber das Stiefmutterproblem*), Beihefte zur Zeitschrift fuer angewandte Psychologie 45, Hamburger Untersuchungen zur Jugend und Sozialpsychologie 1, SIV, 1929; Hildegard Kipp, "Illegitimacy: its Psychological Situation and Problem" (*Die Unehelichkeit: Ihre psychologische Situation und Problematick*), Untersuchungen aus Gross-Berlin, Beihefte zur Zeitschrift fuer angewandte Psychologie 66, Hamburger Untersuchungen zur Jugend-und Sozialpsychologie nr. 4, 1933.

23. Adolf Buseman, ed., "Handbook on Social Environmental Effects for Educators" (*Handbuch zur Paedogogischen*) (Halle [Saale]: H. Schroedel, 1932); Most of Buseman's separate contributions to this field are collected in "Thrity years of Contributions to the Field of Social Environmental Effects of Education," "*Beitrage zur Paedogogischen Milieukunde aus dreissig Jahren,*" (Halle [Salle]: H. Schroedel, 1956).

24. Hildegard Hetzer, "Childhood and Poverty" (*Kindheit und Armut*), 2 Aufl., 1937; (Leipzig: S. Hirzel, 1937) "The development of children in institutions," "*Die Entwicklung des Kindes in der Anstalt,*" in Adolf Buseman, ed. *Handbuch*, pp. 159-73.

25. For a discussion of the activities of Alice Salomon and the psychologists and educators in the German language area see G. Schwaegler, "Family Sociology"; and, G. Wurzbacher, "Sketches of Present-day German Family Life: Methods, Data and Social-educator consequences of a Sociological Analysis of 164 Family Profiles" (*Leitbilder gegenwaertigen*

Deutchen Familienlebens: Methoden, Ergebnisse und soziologischen Analyse von 164 Famillienmonograpgien), 1 ed. (Dortmund: Ardey, 1951; Stuttgart: Enke, 1958, 3ed.); Schwaegler also discusses M. Jahoda, P. F. Lazarsfeld and H. Zeisel, "The Unemployed of Mariental" (*Die Arbeitslosen van Mariental*) (Leipzig: S. Hirzel, 1933).

26. Ernest W. Burgess, "The Family as a Unity of Interacting Personalities," *Family* 7 (1926): 3-9; Willard W. Waller, *The Family, a Dynamic Interpretation* (New York: Dryden, 1938).

NAME INDEX

Abbott, Jacob, 31
Adams, Romanzo, 77
Adler, Felix, 21
Advocacy and Objectivity (Farmer), 5, 10
Alden, Lyman P., 35
Aldous, Joan, xii
Alexander, Thomas, 9
American Civil Engineer, The (Calhoun), 5, 9, 10
American Council on Learned Societies (ACLS), xii
American Journal of Sociology, 42, 55
American Sociological Association, Family Section, viii, xii, 42
American Sociological Review, 8, 10
Ancient Law (Maine), 12, 27
Anderson, Nels, 54, 90
Angell, Robert Cooley, 70, 71, 72, 79, 87, 90
Arner, George Byron, 56
Association for Social Policy, 98, 136
Ayres, Philip W., 34

Bain, Read, 54, 90
Bank, Barbara, 9
Barnes, Harry Elmer, 55, 62
Baum, Marie, 138
Berardo, Felix, xii
Bernard, Jesse, 54
Bevers, A., 137
Blackmar, Frank W., 48, 51, 57, 59
Blake, Nelson Manfred, 29
Bliss, William D. P., 31
Blumer, Herbert, 62
Boas, Frank, 76, 91, 116, 137
Bogue, Donald J., 87
Booth, Charles, 97, 98, 136
Bosanquet, Helen, 57
Brace, Charles Loring, 17, 31-35
Bremmer, Robert H., 31, 34
Brooks, Lee M., 84, 93
Brunner, Edmund DeS., 90
Bruno, Frank J., 54
Buckham, M. H., 30, 32
Buehler, Charlotte, 125, 130
Buehler, Karl, 125, 130
Burgess, Ernest W., ix, xi, 9, 66-70, 72, 81, 87-89, 94, 127, 139
Buseman, Adolf, 125, 138

SUBJECT INDEX

Primary group, xi, 49, 50, 52, 53, 60, 66, 74, 108. *See also* Secondary group; Small group
Problems, 42, 43, 51, 56, 73
Proletariat, 103, 104
Psychiatry, 64, 70, 85, 94
Psychologist, 3, 84
Psychology, 94
Puritan family. *See* Family, Puritan

Questionnaires, 69, 70-72, 76, 77, 83, 102. *See also* Empirical research

Religious education, 31, 41, 44
Research, vii, 6, 40, 51, 57, 68, 69, 71, 83, 88, 89
Role (s), 14, 25, 51, 55, 67, 68, 72, 77, 80, 118, 124, 131
Rural sociology, 73-76, 82, 85, 90, 97

Secondary group, 49, 52
Sex, 15, 69, 77, 81, 86, 94, 101, 104, 122-124
Sexual customs, 15, 28
Small group, 95, 96, 121, 127, 129-131, 134
Socialization, 16, 17, 48-51, 75, 104, 122, 125, 129
Social problems. *See* Problems
Social psychology, xi, 47, 48, 51, 55, 60-64, 66, 70, 85, 123, 125, 127, 133

Social reform, vii, x, 16, 22, 36, 39, 41, 43, 54, 63, 96, 102, 103. *See also* Moral reform
Social sciences, 5, 9-11, 36, 37, 53, 58
Social work(er), x, xi, 5, 10, 20, 26, 40-43, 54-56, 70, 84, 85, 125, 127, 128
Sociologists, ix, 3, 5, 6, 9, 11, 22, 23, 27, 41, 42, 43, 45, 46, 50, 54, 57, 58, 59, 81, 85
Sociology, ix, x, 5, 6, 10, 11, 14, 20, 22-27, 39-48, 50-54, 62, 63, 64, 72, 76, 85, 100, 105, 116, 117-118
Statistics, 23, 24, 32, 36, 43, 46, 54-56, 68, 70, 76, 83, 84, 88, 89, 98, 99, 101, 111, 112, 124, 136, 138
Stepmother, 125
Suicide, 98, 110, 112

Textbooks, 6, 25, 42, 57, 73, 76, 84-86, 90, 93, 114
Theory(-ies), 4, 7, 8, 10, 22, 25, 27, 48, 54, 55, 59, 64, 66, 67, 83, 85, 91, 95-97, 99, 100, 105, 111-113, 115, 117, 122, 123, 126-130, 133-135
Therapy. *See* Counselor

Universities, 39-41
Urbanization, 39, 44, 52, 81, 96, 113, 114
Utopian experiments, 25, 115

About the Authors and Editor

The late RONALD L. HOWARD began this work at the University of Missouri. Selected by the Family Section of the American Sociological Association as a significant contribution to knowledge, the manuscript was revised and edited by Professors Mogey and van Leeuwen after Howard's death.

LOUIS TH. VAN LEEUWEN is Associate Professor of Sociology at Agricultural University in Wageningen, the Netherlands. He is the author of numerous works on marriage and the family.

JOHN M. MOGEY is the 1980-1981 Invitational Professor of Sociology, Arizona State University at Tempe. One of the foremost authorities on family sociology, he is author of *Family and the Neighborhood* and *Rural Life in Northern Ireland*.